THE THREE MOST IMPORTANT EVENTS

THE VITAL ROLES OF THE CREATION,
THE FALL AND THE ATONEMENT IN OUR LIVES

BRUCE E. DANA

spring creek
BOOK COMPANY
Provo, Utah

ISBN 978-1-932898-86-6
e. 1

Published by:
Spring Creek Book Company
P.O. Box 50355
Provo, Utah 84605-0355

www.springcreekbooks.com

Cover design by Nicole Cunningham

Printed in the United States of America
10 9 8 7 6 5 4 3 2 1
Printed on acid-free paper

Library of Congress Control Number: 2008924217

THE THREE MOST IMPORTANT EVENTS

ACKNOWLEDGMENTS

I am forever indebted to my wife, Brenda, for allowing me valuable time to research and write. I am appreciative to all of my family members—whose numbers happily keep increasing—for their constant love and support.

To Matt Erickson, my scholarly friend, for reading this work and giving valuable suggestions so that it will be doctrinally correct.

Special acknowledgement is given to Chad Daybell, of Spring Creek Books, for editing, publishing, and promoting my writings.

TABLE OF CONTENTS

Preface

God, who is the Father of us all, established a plan of salvation whereby his spirit children might progress and become like Him. This plan is called the gospel of Jesus Christ, and it is the only way that mankind can be saved and exalted. The plan consists of the three most important events in all the eternities—the Creation, the Fall, and the Atonement. This work has used the words of scriptures, General Authorities, and noted scholars to explain these most important events that ever have or will occur in eternity.

In my estimation, Elder Bruce R. McConkie is the foremost gospel scholar in the Church. Though other General Authorities have written excellent doctrinal books, none have defined Mormon doctrine as precisely as he did. In addition to being a gifted and prolific writer, he was a true apostolic witness of our Lord. In various writings, he has written so well of these three divine events, which he calls "the three pillars of eternity."

Yet, he, himself, has written these words: "Short of receiving personal revelation on all points, no one author can think of all the meanings or set forth every nuance [awareness of meaning or value] of thought on all points. Further, it seems a waste of literary talent not to preserve some of the thoughts and modes of expression that those . . . who wrote on the same subjects, were led by the spirit of truth to record." Thus, I have freely quoted from this apostolic scholar, and others, in order that the reader will have a more thorough understanding of the Creation, the Fall, and the Atonement.

CHAPTER ONE

The Plan of Salvation

In our quest to become like our Heavenly Father and His Son, Jesus Christ, it is necessary for us to believe and understand the true doctrine of the Creation. However, before we can begin to understand the temporal creation of all things, we must believe and know that God, who is the Father of us all, established a plan of salvation whereby His spirit children might progress and eventually become like Him. As the Prophet Joseph Smith has revealed:

> Who but those who have duly considered the condescension of the Father of our spirits, in providing a sacrifice for His creatures, a plan of redemption, a power of atonement, a scheme of salvation, having as its great objects, the bringing of men back into the presence of the King of heaven, crowning them in the celestial glory, and making them heirs with the Son to that inheritance which is incorruptible, undefiled, and which fadeth not away. . . . How indescribably glorious are these things to mankind![1]

This glorious plan is called the gospel of Jesus Christ. It is the only way that mankind can be saved and exalted. This plan consists of the three most important events in all the eternities: Creation of the earth and man, the Fall of Adam, and the Atonement of Jesus Christ. In this work, we will learn how these three significant events—designated also as the three pillars of eternity—are inseparably woven together to form the Father's plan of salvation.[2]

From what has been revealed, salvation is in Christ and comes because of his atoning sacrifice. He took upon himself the sins of all mankind on conditions of repentance. To gain eternal life—the life that the Father and his Beloved Son have—is the greatest of all the gifts of God. This is available to all because of what Jesus did in Gethsemane and at Golgotha. Thus, immortality and eternal life are gifts of the atonement. Salvation comes because of the Atonement of Jesus Christ; it is the center of the Father's plan of salvation. This redeeming act ransoms mankind from the temporal and spiritual death brought into the world by the fall of Adam and Eve. All will be resurrected because our Lord died and rose again the third day.

Acting under the direction of the Father, Jesus Christ is the Creator of all things. As to His eternal creative acts, Moses was informed: "And worlds without number have I created, and I also created them for mine own purpose; and by the Son I created them, which is mine Only Begotten" (Moses 1:33; see also D&C 76: 20, 23-24). Then this great prophet was told: "*But only an account of this earth, and the inhabitants thereof, give I unto you*" (Moses 1:35, emphasis added). From this we learn that Christ is both the Creator and Redeemer of our world. However, from the writings of Abraham, we are taught that He did not work alone; other "noble and great" spirits assisted Him in this important work (see Abr. 3:22-24).

This study begins by frankly stating we have a very limited knowledge of the creation of this earth and everything associated with it. The Lord has revealed only that portion which we must believe in order to understand the necessity for the Fall and the Atonement. This is all we are obligated to know at this time. Specifically speaking of our world, we are informed that in a future millennial day, "when the Lord shall come [meaning His Second Coming], he shall reveal all things—which no man knew, *things of the earth, by which it was made*, and the purpose and the end thereof" (D&C 101:32-33, emphasis added).

Before we can begin to understand the temporal creation of all things, we must know how our Father became our God. By knowing this doctrine, it will help us understand why He created this earth and all forms of life thereon.

GOD, OUR HEAVENLY FATHER

As to our Heavenly Father's glorified status as an exalted man, as to how he attained his position of supreme prominence, and as to how each of us can pursue the same eternal course and obtain the same exalted destiny, we turn to the Prophet Joseph Smith for knowledge. At the April 7, 1844 conference of the Church held in Nauvoo, Illinois, he preached one of the greatest sermons ever recorded. Before nearly 20,000 members, he revealed the nature and kind of being that God is and told how man, as a joint-heir with our Lord, may become like the Father.[3] In his sermon, the Prophet said:

> I will go back to the beginning before the world was, to show what kind of being God is . . . God himself was once as we are now, and is an exalted man, and sits enthroned in yonder heavens! That is the great secret. If the veil was rent today, and the great God who holds this world in its orbit, and who upholds all worlds and all things by his power, was to make himself visible,—I say, if you were to see him today, you would see him like a man in form—like yourselves in all the person, image, and very form as a man; for Adam was created in the very fashion, image and likeness of God, and received instruction from, and walked, talked and conversed with him, as one man talks and communes with another.[4]

To a majority of the congregation, these were new and surprising teachings. Knowing this, the Prophet explained:

> These are incomprehensible ideas to some, but they are simple. It is the first principle of the Gospel to know for a certainty the character of God, and to know that we may converse with him as one man converses with another, and that he was once a man like us; yea, that God himself, the Father of us all, dwelt on an earth, the same as Jesus Christ himself did; and I will show it from the Bible.[5]

We may safely believe that most of these early Saints did not know that God, our Heavenly Father, once lived on an earth as a mortal man, the same as Jesus did. These truly were marvelous teachings being revealed by the Lord's chosen servant.

Because our Heavenly Father earned His exaltation and was crowned our God by His Heavenly Father and God,[6] He implemented the same eternal plan of salvation that allows His offspring the same opportunity to become like Him. Concerning this teaching, we turn again to the Prophet for understanding:

God himself, finding he was in the midst of spirits . . . saw proper to institute laws whereby the rest could have a privilege to advance like himself. The relationship we have with God places us in a situation to advance in knowledge [the same as our Father has advanced in knowledge]. He has power to institute laws to instruct . . . [his spirit children], that they may be exalted with himself, so that they might have one glory upon another, and all that knowledge, power, glory, and intelligence, which is requisite in order to save them.[7]

"THE ONLY TRUE GOD"

Again from the Prophet, we know that three separate, glorified, and perfected personages comprise the Godhead, or supreme presidency of the universe: God the Father; God the Son; and God the Holy Ghost (first article of faith). We further learn that "the Father has a body of flesh and bones as tangible as man's; the Son also; but the Holy Ghost has not a body of flesh and bones, but is a personage of Spirit" (D&C 130:22).

With this knowledge, we turn our attention to one of the greatest prayers ever recorded in mortality, the Intercessory Prayer, wherein our Lord says: "And this is life eternal, *that they might know thee the only true God*, and Jesus Christ, whom thou hast sent" (John 17:3, emphasis added).

The pattern of prayer given to us by our Lord is that we pray to the Father, in the name of the Son, by the power of the Holy Ghost. Here, Jesus is following this true order—He is praying to His Father, in His own name, and every word is spoken by the power of the Holy Ghost. Accordingly, each member of the Godhead performs an important function and service for mankind. To clarify our Savior's statement, "that they might know thee the only true God," we turn to the expressions of Elder Bruce R. McConkie:

> In the ultimate and final sense of the word, there is only one true and living God. He is the Father, the Almighty Elohim, the Supreme Being, the Creator and Ruler of the universe. . . . Christ is God; he alone is the Savior. The Holy Ghost is God; he is one with the Father and the Son. But these two are the second and third members of the Godhead. The Father is God above all, and is, in fact, the God of the Son. Indeed, the resurrected Christ said to Mary Magdalene: 'I ascend unto my Father, and your Father; and to my God, and your God' (John 20:17).[8]

Each member of the Godhead possesses the same divine nature, knows all things, and has all power. They are united in Their thoughts and actions. Because of Their perfect unity, They are spoken of as being one God (see John 17:21).

Again from the Prophet, we are informed of specific roles within the Godhead: An "everlasting covenant was made between three personages before the organization of this earth, and relates to their dispensation of things to men on this earth; these personages, according to Abraham's record, are called God the first, the Creator; God the second, the Redeemer; and God the third, the witness or Testator."[9]

It is imperative to know that the plan of salvation was ordained by "God the first," who is our Heavenly Father. It is not the plan of Jesus or of Adam or any other of the Father's spirit children. There was only one plan presented. Lucifer desired to amend the Father's plan by depriving agency and seeking the Father's honor in redeeming all of mankind (see Moses 4:1-2).

For mankind in this life, the plan of salvation is the gospel of Jesus Christ. It comprises all the laws, ordinances, and performances that are necessary for our Father's children to gain eternal life and become like Him. This plan is found in the teachings of the "only true and living church upon the face of the whole earth," which is The Church of Jesus Christ of Latter-day Saints (see D&C 1:17-30). Concerning this doctrine, then Bishop Orson F. Whitney said:

> The exclusiveness which the Latter-day Saints exhibit is this: they maintain that the Lord has but one way to save the human race; that the term 'everlasting gospel' is not a misnomer, but means exactly what it says, and that it is eternal as its maker or framer is eternal. It can no more change than He can change. A man [or woman] must obey the same principles now that were obeyed two thousand years ago, or six thousand years ago, or millions of ages ago, in order to attain the presence of His [Jesus Christ's] Father and God [who is our Heavenly Father]. There is but one way, one plan of life and salvation, and there need be but one; for God, being an economist, does not create that which is superfluous; and there can be, in the very nature of things, only one true plan of eternal life.

Bishop Whitney then adds this significant statement:

> Of a necessity God [our Heavenly Father] is the author of perfection; His works are not deficient in any respect, and what He ordains for the salvation of [mankind] is the only way for [mankind] to be saved. Thus it is that the Latter-day Saints preach the everlasting gospel, the unchangeable way of eternal life.[10]

From this statement, we are correctly taught that the Father's plan of salvation is an eternal plan, the same identical plan that allowed our Father to gain His exaltation and become our Heavenly Father. By reason that He is our Heavenly Father, He has declared: "For behold, this is my work and my glory—to bring to pass the immortality and eternal life of man" (Moses 1:39.) We are most thankful that our Father, as a mortal man, proved faithful to the eternal plan of salvation that was operational by His Heavenly Father, the same identical plan used by all the Heavenly Fathers before Him.

In support of this doctrine, the Prophet Joseph Smith said: "If [the Old Testament prophet] Abraham reasoned thus—If Jesus Christ was the Son of God, and John [the Revelator] discovered that God the Father of Jesus Christ had a Father, you may suppose that he had a Father also."[11]

As we notice, the first letter of the word *Father* is capitalized. Though it is true that our Father in Heaven once had an earthly father, the word *Father*, as used by the Prophet, means Heavenly Father. To support this statement, we again use the Prophet's words: "Paul [the New Testament apostle] says that which is earthly is in the likeness of that which is heavenly. Hence if Jesus had a Father [which is also our Heavenly Father], can we not believe that He [our Heavenly Father] had a [Heavenly] Father also? I despise the idea of being scared to death at such a doctrine, for the Bible is full of it."[12]

Revealing fascinating doctrine, the Prophet further declared:

> I want you to pay particular attention to what I am saying. Jesus said that the Father [who is our Heavenly Father] wrought precisely in the same way as His [Heavenly] Father had done before him." Posing it as a question, the Prophet asked, "As the Father had done before?" Answering his own question, he says, "He [our Heavenly Father] laid down His life, and took it up the same as His [Heavenly] Father had done before. He [our Heavenly Father] did as He was sent, to lay down his life and take it up again; and then was committed unto Him [our Heavenly Father] the keys [authority that all Gods receive in order to be a Heavenly Father].[13]

In addition to these profound teachings given by the Prophet Joseph, President Brigham Young declared:

> How many Gods there are, I do not know. But there never was a time when there were not Gods and worlds,

> and when men were not passing through the same ordeals that we are now passing through. That course has been from eternity, and it is and will be to all eternity. You cannot comprehend this, but when you can, it will be to you a matter of great consolation.[14]

In another sermon, President Young provided further insight on this glorious subject:

> It is written, 'Prove all things, hold fast that which is good.' Refuse evil, choose good, hate iniquity, love truth. All this our fathers have done before us; I do not particularly mean Father Adam, or his Father [which is our Heavenly Father[15]]; I do not particularly mean Abraham, or Moses, the Prophets, or Apostles, but I mean our fathers who have been exalted for millions of years previous to Adam's time. They have all passed through the same ordeals we are now passing through.[16]

We are especially thankful that this eternal plan of salvation allows for us the same opportunity, based on our faithfulness, to become like our Heavenly Father!

HEAVENLY MOTHER

With this understanding, logic leads us to the fact that our Father in Heaven is not a single parent. Concerning the doctrine of heavenly parents, Elder McConkie says:

> Implicit in the Christian verity that all men are the spirit children of an *Eternal Father* is the usually unspoken truth that they are also the offspring of an *Eternal Mother*. An exalted and glorified Man of Holiness (Moses 6:57) could not be a Father unless a Woman of like glory, perfection, and holiness was associated with him as a Mother. The begetting of children makes a man a father and a woman a mother whether we are dealing with man in his mortal or immortal state."[17]

Giving further explanation, our apostolic scholar continues:

> This doctrine that there is a *Mother in Heaven* was affirmed in plainness by the First Presidency of the Church (Joseph F. Smith, John R. Winder, and Anthon H. Lund) when, in speaking of preexistence and the origin of man, they said that 'man, as a spirit, was begotten and born of *heavenly parents*, and reared to maturity in the eternal mansions of the Father,' that man is the 'offspring of *celestial parentage*,' and that 'all men and women are in the similitude of the *universal Father and Mother*, and are literally the sons and daughters of deity.' (*Man: His Origin and Destiny*, pp. 348-355).[18]

For purposes of His own, our Heavenly Father has revealed little knowledge of our Heavenly Mother. It is reasonable to believe that no matter the exalted status of the Father, He does not stand alone. By His side, with a glory like unto Him, stands a companion—a glorified, exalted Mother. Concerning a few of Her attributes, we turn to the expressions of President Spencer W. Kimball, twelfth President of the Church: "When we sing that doctrinal hymn and anthem of affection, 'O My Father,' we get a sense of the ultimate in maternal modesty, of the restrained, queenly elegance of our Heavenly Mother, and knowing how profoundly our mortal mothers have shaped us here, do we suppose her influence on us as individuals to be less if we live so as to return there?"[19]

It must be emphasized that all of the godly attributes that our Heavenly Father possesses, the same must be said of our Mother in Heaven. Combined, they are the personification and embodiment of love, truth, and righteousness. Our glorious goal is to become like our Heavenly Parents.

By reason that we pray to our Father in Heaven, some have wondered if it is appropriate to pray also to our Mother in Heaven. To answer, we turn to the words of President Gordon B. Hinckley, then First Counselor to President Ezra Taft Benson:

"There is a tendency for such small beginnings of apostasy to be introduced in our time. We need to be alert to such, to raise the flag of warning and to make correction where necessary.

"For instance, here and there, prayers have been offered to our Mother in Heaven. This started in private prayer, and is beginning to spread to prayers offered in some of our meetings.

"It was Eliza R. Snow who wrote the words: 'Truth is reason, truth eternal, tells me I've a mother there.'

"It has been said that the Prophet Joseph Smith made no correction to what Sister Snow had written. Therefore, we have a Mother in Heaven. Therefore, some assume that we may appropriately pray to her.

"Logic and reason would certainly suggest that if we have a Father in Heaven, we have a Mother in Heaven. That doctrine rests well with me. However, in light of the instructions we have received from the Lord himself, I consider it inappropriate for anyone in the Church to pray to our Mother in Heaven."[20]

MARRIAGE OF OUR HEAVENLY PARENTS

It is without question that our Heavenly Parents are married for time and all eternity. Celestial marriage—whenever and wherever it is performed—is an order of the Melchizedek Priesthood. This patriarchal order allows for a continuation of the family unit throughout eternity.

The Lord, through the Prophet Joseph Smith, has revealed that there are "three heavens or degrees" in the celestial kingdom. In order for a man and a woman to obtain the highest degree, they must enter into this order of matrimony, "meaning the new and everlasting covenant of marriage" (D&C 131:1-2). And, if they are true and faithful to this covenant in mortality, they will have "a continuation of the seeds forever and ever." They will then "be gods, because they have all power" (D&C 132:19-24). Again, the Prophet has revealed that "those who are married by the power and authority of the priesthood in this life," and who are true and faithful to the end, "will continue to increase and have children in the celestial glory."[21]

Because our Heavenly Father implemented a plan of salvation whereby His spirit children may become like Him—the same eternal plan that allowed for His salvation and exaltation—we may be assured that our Heavenly Parents are married by this same "everlasting covenant of marriage" that was revealed to the Prophet. Accordingly, our Heavenly Parents were allowed to have an "eternal increase."

INTELLIGENCES

Though we cannot comprehend the infinite laws of our Heavenly Father, we can visualize Him as personal, loving being who is an exalted, resurrected Man (see D&C 130:22). Using scriptures and words of Church leaders, let us learn how our Heavenly Father has the ability to have three types of offspring: spirit children, immortal children (Adam and Eve), and a mortal child (Jesus Christ).

By revelation, we know that we lived in a pre-earth or premortal state of existence.[22] With the limited knowledge that has been given by the Lord, we are informed that there are two stages of mankind's premortal existence. The first involves a basic or primal element within men and women, which is called "intelligence, or the light of truth" (D&C 93:29).

There are three scriptural references that directly speak of this primal element within mankind. (1) "For man is spirit . . . " (D&C 93:33); (2) "Ye were also in the beginning with the Father; that which is Spirit, even the Spirit of truth." (D&C 93:23); (3) "Man was also in the beginning with God. Intelligence, or the light of truth, was not created or made, neither indeed can be" (D&C 93:29).

Combining these scriptures, the Prophet Joseph gives this explanation, "The spirit of man is not a created being; it existed from eternity, and will exist to eternity. Anything created cannot be eternal."[23] In his King Follett Discourse, the Prophet provides this teaching: "The mind or the intelligence which man possesses is co-equal [meaning co-eternal] with God himself . . .

"I am dwelling on the immortality of the spirit of man . . .

The intelligence of spirits had no beginning, neither will it have an end.

"There never was a time when there were not spirits; for they are co-equal [co-eternal] with our Father in heaven."[24]

It is important to note that nowhere in scripture or any recorded discourse is this primal element of man designated as a living entity in the form and stature of a man or a woman. This primal element is simply designated as "intelligence, or the light of truth," and is directly associated with a substance called "spirit," which is eternal.

In support of this thinking, we turn to the expressions of Elder McConkie: "There is no such thing as an ultimate beginning, a time prior to which there was nothing, any more than there ever can be an ending, a time past which there will be nothing. 'The elements are eternal.' (D&C 93:33) Spirit element (that is, 'the intelligence of spirits') always existed."

Later in his writing, he gives this explanation: "Thus there are two principles: 1. That 'man was also in the beginning with God,' meaning that the spirits of men were created, begotten, and organized, that they came into being as spirits at the time of their spirit birth; and 2. That 'intelligence, or the light of truth, was not created or made, neither indeed can be.' (D&C 93:29), meaning that spirit element, 'the intelligence of spirits,' the substance from which they were created as entities, has always existed and is eternal as God himself. This is the correct meaning and purport of the scriptures and of the Prophet's explanation of the *immortal spirit*, as found in the King Follett Sermon (*Teachings*, pp. 352-354)."[25]

SPIRIT CHILDREN

To differentiate between "intelligence, or the light of truth,"(D&C 93:29), and the term "intelligences" as used by Abraham, as recorded in the Pearl of Great Price, we again turn to our apostolic scholar for clarification: "Abraham used the name *intelligences* to apply to the spirit children of the Eternal Father. The intelligence or spirit element became intelligences after the spirits were born as individuals entities. (Abr.3:22-24)."[26]

All mankind in the premortal existence are the spirit children of our Heavenly Parents. Though we do not know the laws involved, this primal element of "intelligence" was incorporated in the birth of male and female spirit children, wherein they became "intelligences."

The Lord has not revealed the time of gestation for a spirit child, or whether one or several spirit children are born at the time of delivery. Because our Mother in Heaven is a glorified, resurrected Woman, we can properly believe that no pain is associated with giving birth to a spirit child.

What we do know is that the spirit bodies created in the premortal existence have all the body parts of mortal bodies. The brother of Jared first saw the spirit finger of Christ and then was privileged to see His whole spirit body. "I am Jesus Christ," our premortal Lord said. "Behold, this body, which ye now behold, is the body of my spirit; . . . and even as I appear unto thee to be in the spirit will I appear unto my people in the flesh" (Ether 3:14, 16). It is interesting to note that when the brother of Jared saw the finger of the Lord, he said, ". . . for I knew not that the Lord had flesh and blood."

"And the Lord said unto him: Because of thy faith thou hast seen that I shall take upon me flesh and blood" (Ether 3:8-9).

The expression "flesh and blood" means mortality (Lev.17:11; Matt. 16:16-17). Based on the brother of Jared's statement to the premortal Lord, would it be unreasonable to believe that this righteous man's surprise had nothing to do with seeing the form of our Savior's finger, but that our Lord's spirit finger had color or pigmentation, the same as mortals?

To me, it seems unreasonable that spirit children of our Heavenly Parents are born devoid of natural color, for as the revelation to the Prophet Joseph has revealed, ". . . the spirit of man in the likeness of his [mortal] person, as also the spirit of the beast, and every other creature which God has created" (D&C 77:2).

FIRSTBORN SPIRIT

Among all the spirit children of our Heavenly Parents, the firstborn was Jehovah, or Jesus Christ; all others are junior to Him. He has solemnly declared, "I was in the beginning with the Father, and am the Firstborn" (D&C 93:21). Paul, writing to the Colossians, says he is "the image of the invisible God, the firstborn of every creature" (Col. 1:15). In the premortal existence, Jesus had a spirit body, a body composed of spirit element, a body like all of the spirit hosts of heaven. In this spirit realm, He advanced and progressed until He became "like unto God" (Abr. 3:24). It was then that He was foreordained to be the Savior and Redeemer of our world. (see Abr. 3:27; 2 Ne. 2:9; D&C 45:3-5; *Teachings,* p. 190.)

Implicit in the doctrine that Jesus was the firstborn spirit child of our Heavenly Parents is the teaching that there is a lastborn spirit child assigned to our earth.[27] For as the Lord told Moses: "But only an account of this earth, *and the inhabitants thereof,* give I unto you. For behold, there are many worlds that have passed away by the word of my power. . . .

"*And as one earth shall pass away, and the heavens thereof even so shall another come*; and there is no end to my works, neither to my words" (Moses 1:35, 38; emphasis added). Therefore, there are an established number of "inhabitants" assigned to this earth.

TIME IN THE PREMORTAL EXISTENCE

By reason all of mankind are a spirit children of our Heavenly Parents, it is apparent that we all lived for an infinitely long period of time in the premortal existence. There, in this spiritual realm, each of us developed certain aptitudes, gifts, and talents.

In one of his many interesting writings, Elder McConkie penned these thought-provoking words:

> How long did Adam and Abraham and Jeremiah (and all men!) spend in preparing to take the test of a mortal probation? What ages and eons and eternities passed

> away while Christ dwelt in the Eternal Presence and did the work then assigned him? How can we measure infinite duration in finite terms? To such questions we have no definitive answers. Suffice it to say, the passage of time was infinite from man's viewpoint. We have an authentic account, which can be accepted as true, that life has been going on in this system for almost 2, 555,000 years. Presumably this system is the universe (or whatever scientific term is applicable) created by the Father through the instrumentality of the Son.[28]

Regarding this large number of years that have "been going on in this system," Elder McConkie provides this additional, revealing information:

> Joseph Smith and the early brethren in this dispensation knew much that we do not know and will not know until we attain the same spiritual stature that was theirs. This matter of how long eternity has been going on in our portion of created things is one of these matters. The sliver of information that has been preserved for us is found in an epistle of W. W. Phelps, written on Christmas day, 1844, and published to the Church in the *Times and Seasons.* Brother Phelps speaks of 'Jesus Christ, whose goings forth, as the prophets said, have been from of old, from eternity,' in what is a clear allusion to Micah's prophecy that Bethlehem shall be the birthplace of our Lord. 'Out of thee [Bethlehem Ephratah] shall come forth unto me that is to be ruler in Israel; whose goings forth have been from of old, from everlasting,' the Lord said through that ancient prophet. (Micah 5:2) Then, in an interpolative explanation of what is meant by 'from eternity,' or 'from everlasting,' Brother Phelps says, 'And that eternity [the one during which Christ's doings have been known], agreeable to the records found in the catacombs of Egypt, has been going on in this system [not this world], almost two thousand five hundred and

> fifty-five millions of years.' (*Times and Seasons* 5:758.) That is to say, the papyrus from which the Prophet Joseph translated the Book of Abraham, to whom the Lord gave a knowledge of his infinite creations, also contained this expression relative to what apparently is the universe in which we live. . . The time mentioned has no reference, as some have falsely supposed, to the period of this earth's existence.[29]

Our apostolic scholar then concludes by saying:

> Preexistence lasted for a duration beyond our power to understand, and during all the time then involved, the Firstborn and all those who came after him were preparing to take the test of this mortal probation.[30]

From the time of our spirit birth in the premortal existence, each was endowed with agency, and each was subject to the laws ordained by the Father. By obedience to those laws, and by their faithfulness, many were foreordained to become the "noble and great ones" on this earth (see Abr. 3:22-28). This infinitely long period of time in the premortal existence is designated as our "first estate" There, we were told that those "who keep their first estate shall be added upon." This means that the aptitudes, gifts, and talents, each of us developed in this premortal existence would be given in the "second estate," which is mortality on this earth (see Abr. 3:26).

CHRIST CHOSEN AS THE REDEEMER

Many scriptural references state that Christ is the Redeemer (to name a few: Isa.41:14; 54:5; Alma 37:9; 3 Ne. 10:10; D&C 15:1; 18:47). By His exceeding righteousness, He was the mightiest of all the Father's spirit children (see D& C 93:21-23). Concerning His superior advancement, Abraham says "there stood one among" the premortal spirits, "that was like unto God" (Abr.3:24). Accordingly, the Firstborn was called by the Father to be the second member in the Godhead.

To more fully understand how "God the second" is "the Redeemer," we again use the words of Elder McConkie:

> Salvation comes because of Christ and his atoning sacrifice. He is the Redeemer who ransoms men from the effects of Adam's fall. He brings immortality to all men, thus redeeming them from temporal death through the resurrection. Those who believe and obey his laws are redeemed from spiritual death and have eternal life. In like manner he is the Savior. He came 'to save that which was lost' (Matthew 18:11), not to save fallen man in his sins but from his sin.[31]

From this revealed knowledge, we know that Christ is both the Creator and Redeemer of this world. With this introduction, we turn our attention to the creation of our earth and universe.

CHAPTER TWO

The Creation of the Earth and the Universe

Different views of the creation story may be found in Latter-day Saint writings, depending upon the understanding of a particular author. The purpose of this study is to write only what the Lord has revealed either in scripture or by his chosen servants. Though our knowledge is very limited, the Lord has revealed the basic truths which will enable us to understand the true doctrine of creation.

The three accounts of the creation are found in the writings of Abraham, Moses, and the one presented in the temples. Both Abraham and Moses list the creative events on the same successive days. For those familiar with its presentation, the temple account appears to have a different division of events; the six creative days are one continuing period and that there is no one place where the successive events must be placed.[32]

Abraham's account gives a blueprint, as it were, of the Creation. As then Elder Joseph Fielding Smith said: "Abraham gives an account of the *planning* in heaven for this earth and its inhabitants, *before* the work of building was done . . . ."[33]

Therefore, we are informed that the Gods finished Their planning of the creation of all things, for as the record reads: "And thus were their decisions at the time that they counseled among themselves to form the heavens and the earth" (Abr. 5:3).

In addition, Abraham adds this significant statement: "And the Gods came down and formed these the generations of the heavens and of the earth" (Abr. 5:4). Thus, they performed as they had planned; therefore, we can properly consider Abraham's account as an actual creation.

We have no revealed account of the creation of man or other forms of life when they were created as spirits. The statements in Moses 3:5 and Genesis 2:5 are merely interpolations (insertions or interpretations) thrown into the account of the physical creation, meaning that all things were first created in the spirit existence in heaven before they were placed upon this earth.[34]

Scriptures attest that under the direction of the Father, Christ is the creator of this earth. Our Father, Jehovah, Michael, and a host of noble and great spirits assisted in the creative events. The revealed accounts state that the creative events are divided into six days. The work was accomplished as follows:

First Day: The atmospheric heavens and the earth were formed. This orb was "without form, and void" and it was "empty and desolate." The waters of the great deep were present, but "darkness reigned," until the divine decree: "Let there be light." The light and the darkness were then "divided," the one being called "Day" and the other "Night." Thus, our earth was formed and placed in its relationship to our sun (see Moses 2:1-5; Abr. 4: 1-5).

Second Day: "The waters" were "divided" between the surface of the earth and the atmospheric heavens that surround it. A "firmament" or an "expanse" called "Heaven" was created to divide "the waters which were under the expanse from the waters which were above the expanse." Though not written, it appears that provisions were made for clouds and rain to give life to that which will yet grow and dwell on the earth (see Moses 2:6-8; Abr. 4: 6-8).

Third Day: "The waters under the heaven" were "gathered together unto one place, "and the "dry land" appeared. The dry land was called "Earth," and the waters became "the Sea." Grass and herbs and plants and trees came forth. A decree went forth that these items could only grow from "its own seed," and each could only bring forth after its own "kind" (see Moses 2:9-13; Abr. 4:9-13).

Fourth Day: The Gods "organized the lights in the expanse of the heaven" so there would be "seasons" and a way of measuring "days and years." The sun, moon, and stars were given their assigned relationship to the earth (see Moses 2: 14-19; Abr. 4: 14-19).

Fifth Day: Fish and whales and "every living creature" that live in "the waters" came into being. Fowls in all their variety were created. All of these were commanded to "multiply" and bring forth "after their kind" (see Moses 2:20-23; Abr. 4:20-23).

Sixth Day: This was the climax of the creation. First the "beasts of the earth after their kind, and cattle after their kind, and everything which creepeth upon the earth after its kind" were created. Then, as "the Gods," having counseled among themselves, said: "Let us go down and form man in our image, after our likeness." So, God the Father created both the "male and female" and gave them dominion over all created things, and this couple were commanded to multiply and fill the earth with those of their own race. As the "sixth day" closes, the Creators, viewing their labors with satisfaction, see that "all things" which they have "made" are "very good" (see Moses 2:24-31; Abr. 4:24-31).

Regarding the physical creation of the earth, the Prophet says that "the word create came from the word *baurau*, which does not mean to create out of nothing; it means to organize . . . Hence we infer that God had materials to organize the world out of chaos—chaotic matter, which is element, and in which dwells all the glory. Element had an existence from the time he had. The pure principles of element are principles which can never be destroyed; they may be organized and re-organized, but not destroyed. They had no beginning, and can have no end."[35]

As revealed, each creative event is designated as a day; therefore, it is appropriate to wonder what length of time was involved with each. Concerning this subject, the theories of religion and science vary greatly. From Abraham's writings, which were translated by the Prophet Joseph Smith, we are informed that in the "Lord's time" a day is "one thousand years" long, that "one revolution of Kolob" is after the Lord's "manner of reckoning." Abraham was further informed that Kolob governs all those planets which belong to the same order as the earth that Abraham stood upon (see Abr.3:4, 9).

"When this earth was created," says Elder Joseph Fielding Smith, "it was created on celestial time. . . "[36] Prior to Adam's transgression in the Garden of Eden, Abraham saw that Adam's time "was after the Lord's time, which was after the time of Kolob; *for as yet the Gods had not appointed unto Adam his reckoning*" (Abr. 5:13, emphasis added).

Speaking of the six creative days and all that transpired in that time, the Lord says He created "every plant of the field before it was in the earth, and every herb of the field before it grew . . . And I, the Lord God, had created all the children of men; and not yet a man to till the ground; for in heaven created I them" (Moses 3:5).

To clarify, the Lord says, "For I, the Lord God, created all things, of which I have spoken, spiritually, before they were naturally upon the face of the earth. For I, the Lord God, had not caused it to rain upon the face of the earth . . . and there was not yet flesh upon the earth, neither in the water, neither in the air; But I, the Lord God, spake, and there went up a mist from the earth, and watered the whole face of the ground" (Moses 3:5-6).

From a verse in the Doctrine and Covenants, we are informed that when the Lord comes again and the Millennium begins, the earth will return to its paradisiacal state "and all things shall become new" (see D&C 101:25; see also Tenth Article of Faith).

Therefore, we learn that the initial creation was paradisiacal in nature; death and mortality had not yet entered the scene. Concerning this existence, Lehi says, "And all things which were created must have remained in the same state in which they were after they were created; and they must have remained forever, and had no end" (2 Ne.2:22).

CREATION OF EVERY LIVING CREATURE

All that has been revealed concerning the creation of every living creature is this: "And out of the ground I, the Lord God, formed every beast of the field, and every fowl of the air" (Moses

3:19; see also Gen. 2:19). Some have questioned if this is a literal or figurative declaration.

To answer, we read a statement given by President Brigham Young: "When you tell me that father Adam was made as we make adobies [bricks] from the earth, you tell me what I deem an idle tale. When you tell me that the beasts of the field were produced in that manner, you are speaking idle words devoid of meaning."[37]

In conjunction with this statement, Elder Orson F. Whitney said: "Animals do have souls—that is to say, each animal is a spirit and a body, these together constituting the soul; and the same is true of the trees, plants and flowers. They were not formed for any merely temporary purpose, and are to be eternally perpetuated."[38] Just like all of mankind, every living creature on this earth will be resurrected (see D&C 29:23-25; 77:3).

Concerning this doctrine, the Prophet says, "John saw the actual beast in heaven, showing to John that beasts did actually exist there, and not to represent figures of things on the earth . . . beings there of a thousand forms that have been saved from ten thousand times ten thousand earths like this . . . John learned that God glorified Himself by saving all that His hands had made, whether beasts, fowls, fishes or men; and He will glorify Himself with them."[39]

With this revealed knowledge, would we be amiss to say that the Gods allowed a male and female resurrected creature (meaning animals and plants) to reproduce a paradisiacal offspring of every kind assigned to this earth?

As such, these offspring had bodies made of the elements found in the earth—the same elements that allow each to return to dust after their mortal death—as distinguished from the mortal bodies they would receive after the fall.

To support this belief, the Prophet Joseph Smith further revealed: "Where was there ever a son without a father? . . . Wherever did a tree or anything [every living creature] spring into existence without a progenitor? And everything comes in this way."[40]

CREATION OF ADAM AND EVE

The climax of the six creative days was the creation of Adam and Eve. Specifically speaking of Adam it is written: "And I, the Lord God, formed man from the dust of the ground, and breathed into his nostrils the breath of life; and man became a living soul, the first flesh upon the earth, the first man also; nevertheless, all things were before created; but spiritually were they created and made according to my word" (Moses 3:7; see also Gen.2:7-8).

"And the first man of all men have I called Adam," says the Lord, "which is many" (Moses 1:34; 3:7; 6:45; Abr. 1:3). This means that Adam was the first man on this earth and was given the name of "many" to signify the greatness of his posterity.

The scriptural record says that Eve was formed from Adam's rib; whereas Adam exclaimed: "Bone of my bones, and flesh of my flesh; she shall be called Woman, because she was taken out of man (Moses 3:23). After Adam and Eve were formed by the Father, it is written that "they were both naked, the man and his wife, and were not ashamed" (see Gen. 2:25; see also Moses 3:25; Abr. 5:19).

Regarding the word *formed,* Charles W. Penrose, formerly of the First Presidency, has provided this informative meaning: "But we find that we are . . . the children of the great Eternal Father in the spirit, and born here on the earth in the regular order according to the laws of generation, from the time of our father Adam downward, for a purpose; and what is that? That we might obtain a body formed out of these lower elements and through that body be able to obtain experiences that we could not obtain in our first or spiritual estate."[41]

From this explanation, we learn that by the birth process our formed bodies are in the image of God and they contain elements similar to those found in our earth. With this information, we turn our attention to the creation of Adam.

Specifically speaking of the first man on this earth, we learn that the pedigree of Christ was traced by the Apostle Luke to "Enos, which was the son of Seth, which was the son of *Adam, which was the son of God*" (Luke 3:38, emphasis added). To support this pedigree, we read in the book of Moses: "And this is the genealogy of the sons of *Adam, who was the son of God,* with whom God, himself, conversed" (Moses 6:22, emphasis added).

To answer how Adam is a son of God, we turn to a course of study of the Church, *Divine Mission of the Savior,* and read these informative words:

"THE CREATION OF ADAM AND EVE—

"One of the important points about the topic is to learn, if possible, how Adam obtained his body of flesh and bones. There would seem to be but one natural and reasonable explanation, and that is, that Adam obtained his body in the same way Christ obtained his—and just as all men obtain theirs—namely, by being born of woman."[42]

In harmony with this statement, the First Presidency of the Church has written this declarative statement:

"Adam, our great progenitor, 'the first man,' was, like Christ, a pre-existent spirit, and like Christ he took upon him an appropriate body, the body of a man, and so became a 'living soul.' . . . and that all who have inhabited the earth since Adam have taken bodies and become souls in like manner. . . Man began life as a human being, in the likeness of our heavenly father.

"True it is that the body of man enters upon its career as a tiny germ or embryo, which becomes an infant, quickened at a certain stage by the spirit whose tabernacle it is, and the child, after being born, develops into a man. There is nothing in this, however, to indicate that the original man, the first of our race, began life as anything less than a man, or less than the human germ or embryo that becomes a man."[43]

Answering a question sent to the First Presidency, they responded forthrightly: "Your question concerning Adam has not been answered because of pressure of important business . . .

"If you will carefully examine the sermon to which you refer . . .you will discover that . . . President Young denied that Jesus was 'begotten by the Holy Ghost'. . .

"President Young went on to show that our father Adam—that is, our earthly father—the progenitor of the race of man, stands at the head, being 'Michel the Archangel, the Ancient of Days,' and that he was not fashioned from earth like an adobe, but begotten by his Father in Heaven . . . ."[44]

In conjunction with this information, President Brigham Young has revealed this marvelous information concerning those who are valiant in this life and are crowned gods:

"We have not the power in the flesh to create and bring forth or produce a spirit; but we have the power to produce a temporal body. The germ of this, God has placed within us. And when our spirits receive our bodies [at the resurrection], and through our faithfulness we are worthy to be crowned, we will then receive authority to produce both spirit and body."[45]

Now, how do we resolve that Adam is a "son of God" yet Jesus Christ is the "Only Begotten Son" of the Father in the flesh? To answer this intriguing question, we rely upon the apostolic wisdom of Elder McConkie:

"Christ is the Son of God; and he has been so designated from the beginning to show the personal, intimate, family relationship that exists between him and his Father . . .

"Father Adam, the first man, is also a son of God . . . a fact that does not change the great truth that Christ is the Only Begotten in the flesh, for Adam's entrance into this world was in immortality. He came here before death had its beginning, with its consequent mortal or flesh-status of existence."[46]

Elder Russell M. Nelson, a renowned heart surgeon and a member of the Quorum of the Twelve Apostles, has written these informative words: "From the rib of Adam, Eve was formed (see Gen. 2:22; Moses 3:22; Abr. 5:16). Interesting to me is the fact that animals fashioned by our Creator, such as dogs and cats, have thirteen pairs of ribs, but the human being has one less with only twelve. I presume another bone could have been used, but the rib, coming as it does from the side, seems to denote partnership. The rib signifies neither dominion nor subservience, but a lateral relationship as partners, to work and to live, side by side."[47]

In addition, Elder Bruce R. McConkie has written these declarative words concerning Eve: "She was placed on earth in the same manner as was Adam, the Mosaic account of the Lord creating her from Adam's rib being merely figurative (Moses 3:20-25)."[48]

For those who are spiritually ready to accept the truth, we are plainly taught by the Lord's chosen servants that Adam and Eve were naturally begotten and born on this earth by our Heavenly Parents, the same identical way that all men and women in mortality are begotten and born of their earthly parents.

As such, we know how Adam and Eve were "formed" on this world (see Gen. 2:7-8; Moses 3:7). Both were born with a physical but immortal body, upon this earth, from God the Father and our Mother in Heaven. In a future time, Jesus Christ would be born in mortality, upon this earth, from God the Father and the mortal woman, Mary.

From His earthly mother, Mary, our Lord would inherit the ability to die physically because of the blood flowing in His veins; from His Father, Jesus would inherit the power to live forever because of spiritual fluid flowing in His veins. Regarding this teaching, Elder Melvin J. Ballard has given this explanation:

> The nature of the offspring is determined by the nature of the substance that flows in the veins of the being. When blood flows in the veins of the being, the offspring will be what blood produces, which is tangible flesh and bone, but when that which flows in the veins is spirit matter, a substance which is more refined and pure and glorious than blood, the offspring of such beings will be spirit children."[49]

In harmony with this statement, Charles W. Penrose, who was later ordained a member of the Quorum of the Twelve Apostle and a counselor in the First Presidency, has written these words concerning our Savior's resurrection:

> The corruptible blood was purged from the veins [of Jesus Christ], and incorruptible spiritual fluid occupied its place. It was buried a natural body, it was resurrected a spiritual body."[50]

Thus, by laws not revealed, the Father is able to have three types of children: (1) spirit, (2) body form like Adam and Eve, (3) and body form like Jesus Christ. These three types of children are created at different times, and for specific reasons!

The temporal creation of all things on this earth was finished and everything was in a paradisiacal state of existence. Death and mortality, as we know it, was yet to come. Adam and Eve and every living creature had physical bodies that were made of elements found in the earth. Then, the scriptural record concludes with this short but meaningful statement: "Thus the heaven and the earth were finished, and all the host of them. And on the seventh day I, God, ended my work, and all things which I had made . . . and I rested on the seventh day" (Moses 3:1-3).

Admittedly, the revealed accounts of the creation of all things do not correlate with the speculations and theories of science. However, what the inspired word sets forth we are duty-bound to accept.

We conclude our study of the creation by using the words of Elder McConkie:

> He [the Lord] has revealed to us the basic verities which enable us to understand the true doctrine of creation. This doctrine is that the Lord Jesus Christ is both the Creator and the Redeemer of this earth and all that on it is, save only man. It is that the Lord God himself, the Father of us all, came down and created man, male and female, in his own image and likeness. It is that the earth and all else were created in a paradisiacal state so there could be a fall . . . It is that all who accept him as both the Creator and the Redeemer have power to become joint-heirs with him and thereby inherit all that his Father hath.[51]

CHAPTER THREE

The Doctrine of the Fall

The Lord wants us to believe and understand the doctrine of the Fall. This significant event allowed for mortality and procreation and death to transpire on this world. In the wisdom of our Heavenly Father, He created all things on this earth so that they could fall, or change (see 2 Ne. 2:22-25). In order for His children to advance and become like Him, mortal existence was a necessary and important part in the Father's eternal plan of salvation.

It is important to emphasize that we have a very limited knowledge of the Fall and everything associated with it. The Lord has revealed only that portion which we must believe in order to understand the necessity of the Atonement. This is all we are obligated to know at this time. To more fully understand how the Fall transpired, it is necessary to know who Adam and Eve were in the premortal existence.

ADAM AND EVE BEFORE EDEN

Born as a premortal male spirit, Adam, then called Michael, was next in power and authority to Jehovah, the Firstborn.[52] Born as a female spirit, Eve, whose premortal name has not been revealed, was of like stature and intelligence as Adam.

We may safely believe that Jehovah and Michael were friends and companions in righteousness in the premortal existence. Beloved and chosen by the Father, Jehovah, described as being "like unto God," was foreordained to be the Savior and Redeemer of our world (Abr. 3:24). Because of his valiancy, Michael was foreordained to be the first man on this earth. In the war in heaven, Michael, the Archangel, led the armies of heaven when Lucifer and one-third of the spirit host rebelled (Rev. 12:4-9).[53]

We cannot doubt that the greatest of all the female spirits born to our Heavenly Parents was foreordained to be "the mother of the Son of God, after the manner of the flesh" (1 Ne. 11:18). In mortality, this "precious and chosen vessel" would be named "Mary" (Alma 7:10; Mosiah 3:8). Eve, we may safely believe, was second to Mary in righteousness. Because of her valiancy, Eve was foreordained to be "the first of all women" on this earth and "the mother of all living" (Moses 4:26). It is certain that Mary and Eve knew and loved each other, and along with myriads of other faithful daughters of God, labored as diligently, and fought as valiantly in the war in heaven, as did Jehovah, Michael, and all the sons of God.

We may also believe that Adam and Eve knew one another and associated together often in their premortal realm. Due to their close and frequent association, Adam and Eve knew the goodness and quality of each.

PRIESTHOOD GIVEN TO ADAM

As it pertains to Adam, we are taught by the Prophet Joseph Smith that the "Priesthood is an everlasting principle, and existed with God from eternity . . ." Christ is the Great High Priest; Adam next. In addition, we are informed that the "Priesthood was first given to Adam; he obtained the First Presidency, and held the keys of it from generation to generation. He obtained it in the Creation, before the world was formed. . ."[54] (see also Moses 6:64-68.)

GARDEN OF EDEN

Though we are not told when this transpired, the divine word says: "And I, the Lord God, planted a garden eastward in Eden, and there I put the man whom I had formed" (Moses 3:8). After Adam and Eve were formed on this earth by our Heavenly Parents, they both lived in this beautiful place. There are many theories and speculations in the world as to the location of the Garden of Eden. The Lord, through His chosen servants, has identified the exact place. Then Elder Joseph Fielding Smith says:

> We are committed to the fact that Adam dwelt on this American Continent. But when Adam dwelt here, it was not the American Continent, nor was it the Western Hemisphere, for all the land was in *one place*, and all the water was in one place. There was no Atlantic Ocean separating the hemispheres. 'And God said, let the waters under the heaven be gathered together unto *one place*, and let the dry land appear: and it was so. And God called the dry land Earth; and the gathering together of the waters called he Seas: and God saw that it was good.'[55]
> (Gen. 1:9-10.)

In an early Church publication, *Juvenile Instructor*, the following information was written: "From the Lord, Joseph [the latter-day Prophet] learned that Adam had dwelt on the land of America, and that the Garden of Eden was located where Jackson County, Missouri now is."[56] Giving specific information about the exact location, we find that the Temple Block in Jackson County stands on the identical spot where once stood the Garden of Eden.[57]

Thus, this beautiful garden was located on the American Continent "where the City Zion, or the New Jerusalem, will be built," and on August 3, 1831, "the Prophet Joseph Smith dedicated the site for the temple on a spot a short distance west of the court house in Independence, Missouri."[58] (see also D&C 57:1-3.) From this information, we may properly conclude that the boundaries of the Garden of Eden were confined to several acres in a vast land area. In this special place all things were in a state of innocence and beauty (see 2 Ne. 2:22-23).

It is important to emphasize that when Adam and Eve lived in the Garden of Eden they were in the presence of God, and they were taught by Him (Moses 3:15-17). They learned His language, which has been designated in our day as the Adamic language, "a language which was pure and undefiled" (Moses 6:6). According to Elder Joseph Fielding Smith, they were "as familiar with our Eternal Father in that garden as we are with our fathers in mortal life."[59]

While in the garden, the Father commanded "every living creature" to "come unto Adam, to see what he would call them." We may safely believe that by inspiration, Adam gave names to each of them (Moses 3:19-20; see also Abr. 5:20-21).

MARRIAGE OF ADAM AND EVE IN EDEN

While in their paradisiacal state of existence, Adam and Eve were joined together in marriage for time and for all eternity by the power of the everlasting priesthood in the Garden of Eden. (see Gen. 2:24-25; Moses 3:24-25; Abr. 5:18-19). Elder Joseph Fielding Smith says: "Marriage as established in the beginning was an eternal covenant. The first man and the first woman were not married until death should part them, for at that time death had not come into the world. The ceremony on that occasion was performed by the Eternal Father himself whose works endures forever."[60]

CONDITIONS IN THE GARDEN

President John Taylor, third President of the Church, and President Joseph Fielding Smith, then President of the Quorum of the Twelve Apostles, have quoted Elder Parley P. Pratt regarding the condition that prevailed in the Garden of Eden:

> The beasts of the earth were all in perfect harmony with each other; the lion ate straw like the ox, the wolf dwelt with the lamb, the leopard lay down with the kid, the cow and bear fed together, in the same pasture, . . . all was peace and harmony and nothing to hurt nor disturb, in all the holy mountains.

> And to crown the whole, we behold man [Adam] created in the image of God, . . . having dominion over all the vast creation . . . while, at the same time, he inhabits a beautiful and well-watered garden, in the midst of which stood the tree if life, to which he had free access; while he stood in the presence of his Maker [his Father], conversed with Him face to face, and gazed upon His glory, without a dimming veil between. O reader, contemplate, for a moment, this beautiful creation, clothed with peace and plenty; . . . the air swarming with delightful birds, whose never-ceasing notes filled the air with varied melody; and all in subjection to their rightful sovereign, who rejoiced over them; while in a delightful garden, the capital of creation." [61]

TWO SIGNIFICANT TREES

It is written that the Lord "planted the tree of life also in the mist of the garden, and also the tree of knowledge of good and evil" (Moses 3:9). To Adam and Eve this command was given: "Of every tree of the garden thou mayest freely eat, but of the tree of the knowledge of good and evil, thou shalt not eat of it, nevertheless, thou mayest choose for thyself, for it is given unto thee; but, remember that I forbid it, for in the day thou eatest thereof thou shalt surely die" (Moses 3:16-17; see also Abr. 5:11-13). What is meant by partaking of the fruit of the tree of the knowledge of good and evil is that Adam and Eve were given agency to comply with or rebel against the laws ordained by the Father. If they rebelled, their bodies would change from their paradisiacal state of immortality to a state of mortality.

THE SERPENT

To understand how the transgression of Adam and Eve began, we have to first view in the context of the rebellion of Lucifer in the premortal life (see Moses 4:3). The Lord informed Moses that

Lucifer "became Satan, yea, even the devil, the father of all lies, to deceive and blind men, and to lead them captive at his will, even as many as would not hearken unto my voice" (Moses 4:4).

Moses was further told, "And now the serpent was more subtle than any beast of the field which I, the Lord God, had made.

"And Satan put it into the heart of the serpent, (for he [Satan] had drawn away many after him,) and he *sought also to beguile Eve*, for he knew not the mind of God, wherefore he sought to destroy the world" (Moses 4:5-6, emphasis added).

Though this is difficult for us to understand in our mortal state of mind, Satan—by a law allowed by the Lord—spoke "by the mouth of the serpent" to Eve. He asks the woman: "Yea, hath God said—Ye shall not eat of every tree of the garden?" (Moses 4:7).

Evidently Eve was not shocked by the serpent speaking, for she calmly answers: "We may eat of the fruit of the trees of the garden" (Moses 4:8). Then, she gives this qualifying statement about the tree of the knowledge of good and evil: "But of the fruit of the tree which thou beholdest in the midst of the garden, God hath said—Ye shall not eat of it, neither shall ye touch it, lest ye die" (Moses 4:9).

To the woman's answer, the serpent responds: "Ye shall not surely die; for God doth know that in the day ye eat thereof, then your eyes shall be opened, and ye shall be as gods, knowing good and evil" (Moses 4:10-11).

The following description has been written by Brother Hyrum Andrus:

> Upon the scroll of the patriarch Joseph [of Egypt] (which was found with the material from which Joseph Smith translated the Book of Abraham) there was inscribed a representation of the temptation of Eve. Oliver Cowdery wrote: 'The serpent, represented as walking, or formed in a manner to be able to walk, standing in front of, and near a female figure, is to me, one of the greatest representations I have ever seen upon paper, or a writing substance; and must go far towards convincing the rational mind of the correctness and divine authority

> of the holy scriptures. . .' There is also a report that Joseph Smith taught that the serpent had legs and was formed in such a way as to be able to walk, but was later deprived of them in the fall."[62]

With this information, we can conclude that the serpent stood and spoke to Eve about the tree of the knowledge of good and evil. Whether this happened at that particular moment or a short time later, the record says: "And when the woman saw that the tree was good for food, and that it became pleasant to the eyes, *and a tree to be desired to make her wise*, she took of the fruit thereof, and did eat." Once this simple but significant act transpired, we are informed that Eve "gave unto her husband" some of the fruit, "*and he did eat*" (Moses 4:12, emphasis added).

THE TRANSGRESSION OF ADAM AND EVE

It is imperative to remember that while Adam and Eve were living in the garden, they were given this command: "Be fruitful, and multiply, and replenish the earth" (Moses 2:28). While in their immortal state of existence, the man and his wife were incapable of providing mortal bodies for the spirit children of our Heavenly Parents. The Father's plan depended on Adam's and Eve's compliance with this command to be fruitful. If they had disobeyed, they would have lived forever in this paradisiacal Eden, and all the spirit host assigned to this earth would have remained forever in their premortal home. Adam and Eve, and all of mankind, would have been denied the experiences of mortality, of agency, of a resurrection, and of a hope of eternal life to become like our Heavenly Father. Thus, the eternal plan of salvation would have been frustrated, and the purposes of the Father in creating this earth would have been in vain.

Just as the serpent had told Eve, the scriptural record states that after Adam and Eve ate of the fruit the following happened: "*And the eyes of them both were opened*, and they knew that they had been naked"(Moses 4:13, emphasis added). From this information, we may conclude that this change occurred very suddenly.

Concerning Adam partaking of the fruit, Paul says: "And Adam was not deceived, but the woman being deceived was in the transgression" (1 Tim. 2:14). In a revelation, the Lord states:

". . . the devil tempted Adam, and he partook of the forbidden fruit and transgressed the commandment" (D&C 29:40). Various scriptures, as well as apostles and prophets, speak of "Adam's transgression." However, we know that Eve first transgressed and then Adam. Speaking of Adam and Eve partaking of the fruit, Lehi says: "And now, behold, if Adam had not transgressed he would not have fallen, but he would have remained in the garden of Eden." Then he reveals this significant doctrine: "Adam fell that men might be" (2 Ne. 2:22, 25).

While it is true that Adam and Eve partook of the forbidden fruit, whereby they broke a command, they transgressed a lesser commandment in order to obey a higher one. Therefore, it is proper to speak of the *transgression of Adam*, but not the *sin of Adam*. In support of this thinking, Lehi says that Adam and Eve "***knew no sin***" (2 Ne. 2:23, emphasis added). Elder McConkie has written this clarifying explanation: "Knowledge of good and evil is an essential element in the commission of sin, and our first parents did not have this knowledge until after they had partaken of the fruit of the tree of knowledge of good and evil."[63]

THE FALL OF ADAM AND EVE

It appears evident that when Adam and Eve partook of the forbidden fruit, and "the eyes of them both were opened" (Moses 4:13), a dramatic but painless change occurred—blood began to flow in their veins; thus, "they were now quite mortal."[64] By a divine law put in force, "death and mortality entered the world, and the bodies of our first parents were so changed as to permit them to have offspring and thus fulfil the purposes of the Lord in the creation of the earth." (D&C 29:40-44; Moses 5:11; 2 Ne. 2:22-25.)"[65]

After discovering their nakedness, the man and his wife heard the voice of the Father and they hid themselves among the trees of the garden. And God the Father "called unto Adam and said unto him: Where goest thou? . . .

Adam answered truthfully: "I heard thy voice in the garden, and I was afraid, because I beheld that I was naked, and I hid myself."

The Father asked him a two-fold question: "Who told thee thou wast naked? Hast thou eaten of the tree whereof I commanded thee that thou shouldst not eat, if so thou shouldst surely die?"

Trying to justify his action, Adam answered apologetically: "The woman thou gavest me, and commandest that she should remain with me, she gave me of the fruit of the tree and I did eat."

Not responding to Adam, the Father asked Eve: "What is this thing which thou hast done?" Also attempting to shift blame, the woman answered: "The serpent beguiled me, and I did eat" (Moses 4:13-19).

For a wise reason, the serpent was present when the Father questioned Adam and Eve, for the Father "said unto the serpent: Because thou hast done this thou shalt be cursed above all cattle, and above every beast of the field; upon thy belly shalt thou go, and dust shalt thou eat all the days of thy life; and I will put enmity [meaning mutual hatred or ill will] between thee and the woman, between thy seed and her seed; and he shall bruise thy head, and thou shalt bruise his heel" (Moses 4:20-21).

Speaking again to Eve, the Father said: "I will greatly multiply thy sorrow and thy conception. In sorrow thou shalt bring forth children, and thy desire shall be to thy husband, and he shall rule over thee" (Moses 4:22).

Then, to Adam, the Father said: "Because thou has hearkened unto the voice of thy wife, and hast eaten of the fruit of the tree of which I commanded thee, saying—Thou shalt not eat of it, cursed shall be the ground for thy sake; in sorrow shalt thou eat of it all the days of thy life. Thorns also, and thistles shall it bring forth to thee, and thou shalt eat the herb of the field. By the sweat of thy face shalt thou eat bread, until thou shalt return unto the ground—for thou shalt surely die—for out of it wast thou taken: for dust thou wast, and unto dust shalt thou return" (Moses 4:23-25).

Whether this transpired that instant or a short time later, the Father said unto Jehovah: "Behold, the man is become as one of us to know good and evil; and now lest he put forth his hand and partake also of the tree of life, and eat and live forever,

"Therefore I, the Lord God, will send him [meaning both Adam and Eve] from the Garden of Eden, to till the ground from whence he was taken; . . .

"So I drove out the man [and his wife], and I placed at the east of the Garden of Eden, cherubim and a flaming sword, which turned every way to keep the way of the tree of life" (Moses 4:28-31).

Thus, "Adam and Eve were cast from the Garden of Eden in order that they might not partake of 'the tree of life, and eat and live forever.' This means that if they partook of the 'tree of life' which bore a 'celestial fruit' they would pass from mortality into immortality," meaning, "they would die the mortal death, before they had time to obey the first great commandment of bearing children and thereby populating the earth."[66]

This concludes the revealed account of the fall of Adam and Eve. Many in the world believe it is a tragedy that Adam and Eve partook of the forbidden fruit. "Properly understood," says Elder McConkie, "it becomes apparent that the fall of Adam [and Eve] is one of the greatest blessings ever given of God to mankind. It is the way and the means whereby the spirit children of the Father go forth from their celestial home to gain mortal and then immortal bodies. And it provides the way for the experiences, tests, and trials that prepare the faithful for eternal life."[67]

CHAPTER FOUR

Changes Brought by the Fall

EVERY LIVING THING FELL

As was explained earlier in this work, all things were created as spirit entities in the premortal existence (see Moses 3:1-9). When they were placed on this earth, they were immortal, and they would have remained in this state of existence forever (see 2 Ne. 2:22). Every form of life lived in perfect harmony on this world. However, after Adam and Eve partook of the forbidden fruit, the temperament of animals, beasts, fishes, and fowl changed. To obtain food, the animal kingdom began to prey upon each other. By reason of the fall, enmity, conflict, pain, sickness, and death were introduced into the world.

We know that Adam and Eve were to obtain their food and clothing by the sweat of their brows (see Moses 5:1). They, too, could eat meat and were commanded to "offer the firstlings of their flocks" (see Moses 5:5). In our day, the Lord has declared: "For, behold, the beasts of the field and the fowls of the air, and that which cometh of the earth, is ordained for the use of man for food and for raiment" (D&C 49:19).

Animals and fowls and fishes were now allowed to produce after their kind, and each was subject to disease and death. Likewise, vegetation, grasses, trees, and a variety of plant life in the waters were allowed to produce after their kind. They, too, were subject to disease and death (see Moses 2:20-25). Thorns, thistles, and weeds were allowed to grow and afflict and torment mankind (see Moses 4:23-25). Various reptiles were allowed to inflict pain and suffering (see Moses 4:20-21). Truly, the fall brought mortality to the world with all of its attendant blessings and challenges. All of this was an essential and necessary part of the Father's plan of salvation.

RECKONING OF TIME CHANGED

Once Adam and Eve were cast from the Garden of Eden, they were no longer living under celestial time, governed by Kolob, but were placed under a different system of time (see Abr. 3:4-9; 5:13). Though their time may not have been calculated as we do today, we know that they described a certain number of days as a year. In the Biblical record, we read: "And all the days that Adam lived were nine hundred and thirty years: and he died" (Gen. 5:5).

WAS THE LOCATION OF THE EARTH CHANGED?

Some have wondered if the location of the earth was changed after the transgression of Adam and Eve. In an early Church newspaper, the following was written in an article:

> The earth no longer retained its standing in the presence of Jehovah; but was hurled into the immensity of space; and there to remain till it has filled up the time of its bondage to sin and Satan. It was immediately cursed, and Adam and Eve were obliged to procure their food and raiment by the sweat of their brow. The beasts became ferocious, and went prowling about the wilderness seeking the inferior animals for a prey. . . . [68]

Based on this statement, a few LDS scholars have surmised that in order to change the reckoning of time, our earth necessitated a removal from near Kolob to our present solar system. Elder McConkie, who is considered one of the greatest scholars of the

Church, has taken a differing view. Concerning the creation of this earth and universe, he has written the following:

> *The First Day*—Elohim, Jehovah, Michael, a host of noble and great ones—all these played their parts. 'The Gods' created the atmospheric heavens and the temporal earth. It was 'without form, and void'; as yet it could serve no useful purpose with respect to the salvation of man. It was 'empty and desolate'; life could not exist on its surface; it was not yet a fit abiding place for those sons of God who shouted for joy at the prospect of a mortal probation. The 'waters' of the great 'deep' were present, and 'darkness reigned' until the divine decree: 'Let there be light.' The light and the darkness were then 'divided,' the one being called 'Day' and the other 'Night.' Clearly our planet was thus formed as a revolving orb and placed in its relationship to our sun. (see Moses 2:1-5; Abr. 4:1-5).[69]

The important thing to remember is that the Lord can change the reckoning of time on our earth—or anything for that matter—by simply giving a divine command. To illustrate: The Gods said, "Let there be light," and "there was light" (see Moses 2:3; Abr. 4:3).

WHERE ADAM AND EVE LIVED AFTER EDEN

Concerning significant events that have transpired in the State of Missouri in our day, Elder Alvin R. Dyer has written the following: "As to how [Adam and Eve] ended in the valley of Adam-ondi-Ahman, which is approximately 90 miles to the north and east [of the Garden of Eden], we may consider the following statement:

"'Adam-ondi-Ahman was at the point where Adam came and settled and blessed his posterity after being driven from the Garden of Eden. This was revealed through Joseph Smith the Prophet . . . When Adam and Eve were driven from the Garden they traveled in a northeasterly course until they came to a valley on the east side of the Grand River.'

"The fact that Adam-ondi-Ahman is clearly identified in the revelations which is to the north of Jackson County is conclusive. (See D&C Section 116)." [70]

From this information, we can conclude that by divine providence, Adam and Eve were inspired to travel a considerable distance to live in a special valley. "As near as we can judge," says Elder McConkie, "and this view comes down from the early brethren who associated with the Prophet Joseph Smith, who was the first one to use the name in this dispensation—Adam-ondi-Ahman means the place or land of God where Adam dwelt."[71]

Continuing, our apostolic scholar explains: "Apparently the area included was a large one; at least, the revelations speak of the *land*, the *valley*, and the *mountains* of Adam-ondi-Ahman. They tell us that Christ himself 'established the foundations of Adam-ondi-Ahman' (D&C 78:15-16), and that it included the place now known as Spring Hill, Daviess County, Missouri. (D&C 116.)'

"Far West, Missouri, also appears to be included in the land of Adamn-ondi-Ahman . . ."[72]

Concerning the significance of this valley, Elder McConkie provides this information: "One of the greatest spiritual gatherings of all the ages took place in the Valley of Adam-ondi-Ahman some 5,000 years ago, and another gathering—of even greater importance relative to this earth's destiny—is soon to take place in that same location."[73] (see also D&C 107:53-56; Dan. 7:19-24; *Teachings*, 157.)

ADAM AND EVE WERE TAUGHT THE GOSPEL

A short time after Adam and Eve had been driven from the Garden of Eden, wherein they had died a spiritual death, meaning they were cut off from the presence of God the Father, Jehovah began to reveal to them the gospel of Jesus Christ. This was not revealed all at once, but line upon line.

It is written that "Adam knew his wife, and she bare unto him sons and daughters, and they began to multiply and to replenish the earth. And from that time forth, the sons and daughters of Adam began to divide two and two in the land, and to till the land, and to tend flocks, and they also begat sons and daughters" (Moses 5:2-3).

Though we have a limited understanding of all that was involved, we are informed that after the Fall, "Adam and Eve, his wife, called upon the name of the Lord, and they heard the voice of the Lord . . . speaking unto them, and they saw him not; for they were shut out from his presence" (Moses 5:4). Accordingly, the man and his wife had experienced a spiritual death. It is important to emphasize that both Adam and Eve prayed; both heard the voice of the Lord; and both were commanded to worship Him.

Our first parents were also commanded to "worship the Lord their God, and should offer the firstlings of their flocks, for an offering unto the Lord" (Moses 5:5). Adam and Eve were obedient to this command.

After a time, an unnamed angel appeared unto Adam and asked: "Why dost thou offer sacrifices unto the Lord? And Adam said unto him: I know not, save the Lord commanded me" (Moses 5:6).

Foretelling a future day when the mortal Lord will be crucified on the cross, this angelic ministrant explained: "This thing is a similitude of the sacrifice of the Only Begotten of the Father, which is full of grace and truth" (Moses 5:7). Giving further instructions, the angel declared: "Wherefore, thou shalt do all that thou doest in the name of the Son [meaning the Son of God], and thou shalt repent and call upon God in the name of the Son forevermore" (Moses 5:8).

Whether it happened that day, or short time later, the scriptural record says that "the Holy Ghost fell upon Adam," and Adam prophesied many things (Moses 5:9-10).

Adam told his wife all that had transpired, and in response to this information, "Eve . . . was glad, saying: Were it not for our transgression [of eating the forbidden fruit and being driven from the Garden of Eden] we never should have had seed, and never should have known good and evil, and the joy of our redemption, and the eternal life which God giveth unto all the obedient" (Moses 5:11).

Then, Adam and Eve "blessed the name of God," began to teach the gospel to their posterity, and continued in prayer and devotion and sacrifice the rest of their mortal life" (see Moses 5:12; 6:1).

ADAM AND EVE GIVEN TIME TO REPENT

While speaking to his son Corianton, Alma says that "after the Lord God sent our first parents forth from the garden . . . that there was a time granted unto man [meaning Adam and Eve and all mankind] to repent, yea, a probationary time, a time to repent and serve God.

"For behold, if Adam had put forth his hand immediately, and partaken of the tree of life, he would have lived forever . . . having no space for repentance; yea, and also the word of God would have been void, and the great plan of salvation would have been frustrated.

"But behold, it was appointed unto man to die . . . and man became lost forever, yea, they became fallen man.

"And now, ye see by this that our first parents were cut off both temporally and spiritually from the presence of the Lord; and thus we see they became subjects to follow after their own will" (Alma 42:2, 4-7).

ADAM AND EVE FORGIVEN THEIR TRANSGRESSION

Speaking by divine investiture of authority for the Father, Jehovah said to Adam: "I am God; I made the world, and men before they were in the flesh. . . . If thou wilt turn unto me, and hearken unto my voice, and believe, and repent of all thy transgressions, and be baptized, even in water, in the name of mine Only Begotten

Son . . . which is Jesus Christ, the only name which shall be given under heaven, whereby salvation shall come unto the children of men, ye shall receive the gift of the Holy Ghost, asking all things in his name, and whatsoever ye shall ask, it shall be given you" (Moses 6:51-52).

Thus, mankind must repent and be baptized and receive the Holy Ghost to gain salvation. With this stated, we turn our attention to Adam. Desiring to obtain information, Adam asked: "Why is it that men must repent and be baptized in water?" Answering, Jehovah said: "*Behold, I have forgiven thee [and Eve] thy transgression in the Garden of Eden.*"

"Hence came the saying abroad among the people, that the Son of God hath atoned for original guilt, wherein the sins of the parents cannot be answered upon the heads of the children, for they are whole from the foundations of the world" (Moses 6:53-54, emphasis added).

ADAM AND EVE WERE BAPTIZED

Continuing to instruct Adam, the Lord revealed the following gospel principles: "Wherefore teach it unto your children, that all men, everywhere, must repent, or they can in nowise inherit the kingdom of God, for no unclean thing can dwell there, or dwell in his presence" (Moses 6:57).

"By reason of transgression cometh the fall, which fall bringeth death, and inasmuch as ye were born into the world by water, and blood, and the spirit [meaning being born as all mankind are born], . . . even so ye must be born again into the kingdom of heaven, of water, and of the Spirit, and be cleansed by blood, even the blood of mine Only Begotten . . .

"For by the water [of baptism by immersion] ye keep the commandment; by the Spirit [of receiving the Holy Ghost by the laying on of hands] ye are justified, and by the blood [from the sacrifice of Jesus Christ] ye are sanctified . . .

"And now, behold, I say unto you: This is the plan of salvation unto all men, through the blood of mine Only Begotten, who shall come in the meridian of time" (Moses 6:59-60, 62).

Though we are not told when this event happened, we are informed that "when the Lord had spoken with Adam . . . that Adam cried unto the Lord, and he was caught away by the Spirit of the Lord, and was carried down into the water, and was laid under the water, and was brought forth out of the water.

"*And thus he was baptized*, and the Spirit of God descended upon him, *and thus he was born of the Spirit*, and became quickened in the inner man.

"And he heard a voice out of heaven, saying, Thou art baptized with fire, and with the Holy Ghost. This is the record of the Father, and the Son, from henceforth and forever" (Moses 6:64-66, emphasis added).

It is without question that Eve—along with many of their posterity—was also baptized and received the gift of the Holy Ghost. More than likely this was performed by Adam, who held the priesthood and authority to perform these necessary and important ordinances (see *Teachings*, 157; D&C 13:1; 20:38-43, 68-74; 84:26-27).

Thus, mortality and procreation, spiritual and temporal death, of trials and probation, of hearing anew the gospel of Jesus Christ—all of these things became available to mankind with the changes that occurred after the fall of Adam and Eve.

CHAPTER FIVE

The Atonement

The Atonement of Jesus Christ is the most important event that has occurred or ever will occur in all eternity. This transcendent act paid the ransom to reclaim mankind, and all created things, from the effects of the Fall of Adam and Eve. Salvation is in Christ and was accomplished because of His atoning sacrifice. Every living thing will be resurrected because our blessed Lord died and rose again. Though we have a limited understanding of how it was accomplished, the Atonement of our Lord ransoms mankind from temporal and spiritual death brought by the Fall.

DOCTRINE OF THE ATONEMENT

The doctrine of the Atonement is the foundation upon which all gospel truths rest. The Prophet Joseph Smith has said that "all other things which pertain to our religion are only appendages to it."[74] While recording a glorious vision, the Prophet wrote: "And this is the gospel . . . that he came into the world, even Jesus, to be crucified for the world, and to bear the sins of the world, and to sanctify the world, and to cleanse it from all unrighteousness; that through him all might be saved whom the Father had put into his power and made by him" (D&C 76:40-42).

In complete harmony, the resurrected Lord said to His Nephite disciples: "Behold I have given unto you my gospel, and this is the gospel which I have given unto you—that I came into the world to do the will of my Father, because my Father sent me. And my Father sent me that I might be lifted up upon the cross" (3 Ne. 27:13-14).

Thus, salvation and redemption comes because of the Atonement of our Lord Jesus Christ. Without this divine act, the Father's plan of salvation would have been frustrated and the whole purpose of creating and populating this earth would be void. Because our Savior took upon Himself the burden of the sins of mankind, all are assured of a hope of the highest exaltation in the hereafter, based upon their faithfulness (see D&C 76).

KNOWLEDGE REVEALED BY AN ANGEL

While addressing his people, King Benjamin related this doctrine of the Atonement as revealed by an angel from heaven: ". . . as in Adam, or by nature, they fall, even so the blood of Christ atoneth for their sins. And moreover, I say unto you, that there shall be no other name given nor any other way nor means whereby salvation can come unto the children of men, only in and through the name of Christ, the Lord Omnipotent.

"For behold he judgeth, and his judgment is just; . . . salvation was, and is, and is to come, in and through the atoning blood of Christ, the Lord Omnipotent.

"For the natural man is an enemy to God, and has been from the fall of Adam, and will be, forever and ever, unless he yields to the enticings of the Holy Spirit, and putteth off the natural man and becometh a saint through the atonement of Christ the Lord, and becometh as a child, submissive, meek, humble, patient, full of love, willing to submit to all things which the Lord seeth fit to inflict upon him, even as a child doth submit to his Father" (Mosiah 3:16-19).

Providing further knowledge, Moroni taught that God "created Adam, and by Adam came the fall of man.

"And because of the fall of man came Jesus Christ, even the

Father and the Son; and because of Jesus Christ came the redemption of man. And because of the redemption of man, which came by Jesus Christ, they are brought back into the presence of the Lord; yea, this is wherein all men are redeemed, because the death of Christ bringeth to pass the resurrection, which bringeth to pass a redemption from an endless sleep, from which sleep all men shall be awakened by the power of God when the trump shall sound; and they shall come forth, both small and great, and all shall stand before his bar, being redeemed and loosed from this eternal band of death, which death is a temporal death.

"And then cometh the judgment of the Holy One upon them; and then cometh the time that he that is filthy shall be filthy still; and he that is righteous shall be righteous still; he that is happy shall be happy still; and he that is unhappy shall be unhappy still" (Morm. 9:12-14).

In our day, the Lord says that because of his Atonement, and following the "natural death," mankind is "raised in immortality unto eternal life, even as many as would believe; and they that believe not unto eternal damnation; for they cannot be redeemed from their spiritual fall, because they repent not" (D&C 29:43-44). It is important to emphasize that those who have not arrived at the years of accountability, either physically or mentally, are saved in the celestial kingdom by virtue of the Lord's Atonement. It is written: ". . . little children are whole, for they are not capable of committing sin, wherefore the curse of Adam is taken from them in me, that it hath no power over them" (Moro. 8:8; D&C 29:46-47; *Teachings*, 107).

"When the prophets speak of an infinite atonement," says Elder McConkie, "they mean just that. Its effects cover all [mankind], the earth itself and all forms of life thereon, and reach out into the endless expanses of eternity . . .

"Because of the atonement and by obedience to gospel law [mankind] have power to become the sons of God in that they are spiritually begotten of God and adopted as members of his family. They become the sons [and daughters] of God and joint-heirs with Christ of the fulness of the Father's kingdom."[75]

GARDEN OF GETHSEMANE

To more fully understand how the Atonement of our Lord was accomplished, we turn our attention to events that occurred after the Last Supper was eaten by Jesus and His chosen apostles. John says that Jesus "went forth with his disciples over the brook Cedron, where was a garden, into the which he entered, and his disciples." Then, these explanatory words are written: "And Judas [Iscariot] also, which betrayed him, knew the place: for Jesus ofttimes resorted thither with his disciples" (John 18:1-2).

Regarding this scene, Elder James E. Talmage has written this description:

> Jesus and the eleven apostles went forth from the house in which they had eaten, passed through the city gate, which was usually left open at night during a public festival, crossed the ravine of the Cedron, or more accurately Kidron, brook, and entered an olive orchard known as Gethsemane, on the slope of Mount Olivet." Then, in an endnote, he adds: "The name [Gethsemane] means 'oil-press' and probably has reference to a mill maintained at the place for the extraction of oil from the olives there cultivated. John refers to the spot as a garden, from which designation we may regard it as an enclosed space of private ownership.[76]

We cannot with surety reconstruct the events that transpired that evening in the Garden of Gethsemane; however, as close as we can, we will present what has been written by the gospel writers. Mark says that Jesus said to eight of his disciples: "Sit ye here, while I shall pray" (Mark 14:32). According to Luke's gospel, he further instructed them: "Pray that ye enter not into temptation" (Luke 22:40).

As was the case with the raising of the daughter of Jairus and on the Mount of Transfiguration, Jesus took only Peter, James, and John farther into the garden. At a certain spot, our Lord told the three presiding apostles: "My soul is exceeding sorrowful, even unto death; tarry ye her and watch" (Mark 14:34; see also Matt.

26:38). Matthew wrote that Jesus "went a little further, and fell on his face, and prayed" (Matt. 26:39). Mark says that our Lord "went forward a little, and fell on the ground [prostrated himself], and prayed" (Mark 14:35). Luke wrote that He withdrew from the three apostles "about a stone's cast, and kneeled down, and prayed" (Luke 22:41). Thus, from these gospel narratives, we may safely believe that our beloved Lord may have done each of these things throughout the evening of His greatest agony.

Before Peter, James, and John slept, one or all heard a portion of the prayer offered by our Lord. Matthew says: "O My Father, if it be possible, let this cup pass from me: nevertheless not as I will, but as thou wilt" (Matt. 26:39).

The testimony of Mark reads: "Abba, Father, all things are possible unto thee; take away this cup from me: nevertheless not what I will, but what thou wilt" (Mark 14:36).

Luke's version: "Father, if thou be willing, remove this cup from me: nevertheless not my will, but thine, be done" (Luke 22:42). He further informs us that "there appeared an angel unto him from heaven, strengthening him" (Luke 22:43).

AN ANGEL APPEARED TO JESUS

Concerning this angel, Elder McConkie has written these thought-provoking words:

> The angelic ministrant is not named . . . and if we might indulge in speculation, we would suggest that the angel who came into this second Eden [which is the Garden of Gethsemane] was the same person who dwelt in the first Eden. At least Adam, who is Michael, the archangel—the head of the whole heavenly hierarchy of angelic ministrants—seems the logical one to give aid and comfort to his Lord on such a solemn occasion. Adam fell, and Christ redeemed men from the fall; theirs was a joint enterprise, both parts of which were essential for the salvation of the Father's children.[77]

JESUS SWEAT GREAT DROPS OF BLOOD

Luke writes: "And being in an agony [Jesus] prayed more earnestly: and his sweat was as it were great drops of blood falling down to the ground" (Luke 22:44).

"And as to the blood that oozed from his pores," writes Elder McConkie, "we cannot do better than recall the words of the angelic ministrant, spoken to the Nephite Hebrew, Benjamin: 'And Lo, he shall suffer temptations, and pain of body, . . . even more than man can suffer, except it be unto death; for behold, blood cometh from every pore, so great shall be his anguish for the wickedness and the abominations of his people (Mosiah 3:7)."[78]

"And when he rose up from prayer," Luke continues, "and was come to his disciples [Peter, James, and John], he found them sleeping for sorrow" (Luke 22:45). And Jesus said unto them, "Why sleep ye? rise and pray, lest ye enter into temptation" (Luke 22:46). Mark adds this information: "Simon, sleepest thou? couldest not thou watch one hour? Watch ye and pray, lest ye enter into temptation." (Mark 14:37-38). To this question, the three presiding apostles answered our Lord: "The spirit truly is ready, but the flesh is weak" (Joseph Smith Translation Mark 14:43).

Jesus left these three again and prayed: "O my Father, if this cup may not pass away from me, except I drink it, thy will be done" (Matt. 26:42). Returning, our Lord found them sleeping again, from which we may safely believe that Jesus had been away for a length of time and had offered many prayerful words to His Father. When He returned again to His chosen three He "found them asleep again . . . neither wist they what to answer him" (Mark 14:40). Jesus went away and prayed a third time, "saying the same words" (Matt. 26:44). Returning for the last time, our Lord said to the three, "Sleep on now, and take your rest" (Matt. 26:45). After finishing their sleep, Jesus said to His presiding apostles, "Rise up, let us go; lo, he that bretrayeth me is at hand" (Mark 14:42). Thus, ends the accounts by the gospel writers of the suffering of our Lord in Gethsemane.

THE MYSTERY OF REDEMPTION

Elder McConkie has penned these truthful words:

> There is no mystery to compare with the mystery of redemption, not even the mystery of creation. Finite minds can no more comprehend how and in what manner Jesus performed his redeeming labors than they can comprehend how matter came into being, or how Gods began to be. Perhaps the very reason Peter, James, and John slept was to enable a divine providence to withhold from their ears, and seal up from their eyes, those things which only Gods can comprehend."[79]

WHERE THE ATONING SACRIFICE TOOK PLACE

Concerning where the atoning sacrifice of the Lord took place, Elder McConkie again has penned these words:

> Where and under what circumstances was the atoning sacrifice of the Son of God made? Was it on the Cross of Calvary or in the Garden of Gethsemane? It is to the Cross of Christ that most Christians look when centering their attention upon the infinite and eternal atonement. And certainly the sacrifice of our Lord was completed when he was lifted up by men; also, that part of his life and suffering is more dramatic and, perhaps, more soul stirring. But in reality the pain and suffering, the triumph and grandeur, of the atonement took place primarily in Gethsemane.

He further explains:

> It was there Jesus took upon himself the sins of the world on conditions of repentance. It was there he suffered beyond human power to endure. It was there he sweat great drops of blood from every pore. It was there

> his anguish was so great he fain would have let the bitter cup pass. It was there he made the final choice to follow the will of the Father. It was there that an angel from heaven came to strengthen him in his greatest trial. Many have been crucified and the torment and pain is extreme. But only one, and he the Man who had God as his Father, has bowed beneath the burden of grief and sorrow that lay upon him in that awful night, that night in which he descended below all things as he prepared himself to rise above them all."[80]

Fifty years earlier, Elder Talmage wrote these powerful words concerning the atoning sacrifice of our Lord:

> Christ's agony in the garden is unfathomable by the finite mind, both as to intensity and cause. . . . He struggled and groaned under a burden such as no other being who has lived on earth might even conceive as possible. It was not physical pain, nor mental anguish alone, that caused Him to suffer such torture as to produce an extrusion of blood from every pore; but a spiritual agony of soul such as only God was capable of experiencing. No other man, however great his powers of physical or mental endurance, could have suffered so; for his human organism would have succumbed, and syncope would have produced unconsciousness and welcome oblivion . . . .

He further explains:

> In some manner, actual and terribly real though to man incomprehensible, the Savior took upon Himself the burden of the sins of mankind from Adam to the end of the world. Modern revelation assists us to a partial understanding of the awful experience. In March 1830, the glorified Lord, Jesus Christ, thus spake: 'For behold, I, God, have suffered these things for all, that they might not suffer if they would repent, but if they would not repent, they must suffer even as I, which suffering caused

> myself, even God, the greatest of all, to tremble because of pain, and to bleed at every pore, and to suffer both body and spirit: and would that I might not drink the bitter cup and shrink—nevertheless, glory be to the Father, and I partook and finished my preparations unto the children of men.' (D&C 19:16-19)

He then concludes:

> From the terrible conflict in Gethsemane, Christ emerged a victor. Though in the dark tribulation of that fearful hour He had pleaded that the bitter cup be removed from His lips, the request, however oft repeated, was always conditional; the accomplishment of the Father's will was never lost sight of as the object of the Son's supreme desire. The further tragedy of the night, and the cruel inflictions that awaited Him on the morrow, to culminate in the frightful tortures of the cross, could not exceed the bitter anguish through which He had successfully passed.[81]

ATONEMENT COMPLETED ON THE CROSS

While our beloved Lord hung on the tortuous cross, He spoke seven times. During the fourth utterance, He "cried with a loud voice, saying, Eli, Eli, lama sabachthani? that is to say, My God, my God, why hast thou forsaken me?" (Matt. 27:46; Mark 15:34). This expression uses the same words as the Messianic prophecy found in Psalm 22:1. Concerning this, Elder Talmage wrote these meaningful words:

> What mind of man can fathom the significance of that awful cry? It seems, that in addition to the fearful suffering incident to crucifixion, the agony of Gethsemane had recurred, intensified beyond human power to endure. In that bitterest hour the dying Christ was alone, alone in

> most terrible reality. That the supreme sacrifice of the Son might be consummated in all its fulness, the Father seems to have withdrawn the support of His immediate Presence, leaving to the Savior of men the glory of complete victory over the forces of sin and death.[82]

Elder McConkie writes these equally moving words:

> The infinite and eternal atonement has now been wrought. Jesus has gained the victory; he has done all that his Father sent him to do; now he faces only the physical agonies of the cross, and he can think of his own bodily needs. He calls out, 'I thirst,' and these are the fifth words from the cross . . . As he drank, the heartless among them called out: 'Let him alone; let us see whether Elias will come to take him down.' At Jesus' behest Elijah and twelve legions of angels would have attended the cross at any time; at his word heaven and earth would pass away; by his voice nothing was impossible—and yet there was no divine intervention. Our Pattern, our Prototype, our Exemplar marked the path for all men. He endured to the end . . .

He then concludes:

> Thereupon Jesus made his final earthly report to the one who had sent him. 'Father, it is finished, thy will is done,' he said; and this is the sixth utterance from the cross. How, then, does a God die? It is a voluntary act; no man taketh his life from him; he lays it down of himself; he has power to lay it down and power to take it again. Jesus makes his seventh utterance from the cross. He says simply: 'Father, into thy hands I commend my spirit,' . . . 'And having said thus, he gave up the ghost.' [83]

Though Jesus voluntarily yielded up His life, there was a direct physical cause of death. Elder Talmage has provided this explanation:

> The strong, loud utterance, immediately following which He bowed His head and 'gave up the ghost,' when considered in connection with other recorded details, points to a physical rupture of the heart as the direct cause of death. If the soldier's spear was thrust into the left side of the Lord's body and actually penetrated the heart, the outrush of 'blood and water' observed by John [19:34] is further evidence of a cardiac rupture; for it is known that in the rare instances of death resulting from a breaking of any part of the wall of the heart, blood accumulates within the pericardium, and there undergoes a change by which the corpuscles separate as a partially clotted mass from the almost colorless, watery serum . . .

He then concludes with his personal belief:

> The present writer [Elder Talmage] believes that the Lord Jesus died of a broken heart. The psalmist sang 'Reproach hath broken my heart; and I am full of heaviness . . . .' (Psalm 69:20-21; See also 22:14) [84]

THE RESURRECTION OF OUR LORD

It is now Sunday, the first day of the week. Our beloved Lord had been dead three days. Elder McConkie, who is quoting Alfred Edersheim, a Jewish scholar, has written:

> According to Jewish tradition, 'the soul hovered round the body till the third day, when it finally parted from its earthly tabernacle,' and it was on that day that 'corruption was supposed to begin.' Up to that time relatives and friends were in the habit of 'going to the grave, . . . so as to make sure that those laid there were really dead.' [85]

According to John's record, "when it was yet dark," Mary Magdalene went to the sepulchre where Jesus was laid. Arriving at this garden tomb, this loving and devoted disciple found the stone taken away from the sepulchre, "and two angels sitting thereon"

(Joseph Smith Translation Mark 20:1). We may properly believe that she looked in and found an empty tomb. Without hesitation, she ran to Peter, and to John, and told them: "They have taken away the Lord out of the sepulchre, and we know not where they have laid him." Peter and John "ran both together: and the other disciple [who is John] did outrun Peter, and came first to the sepulchre. And he stooping down, and looking in, saw the linen clothes lying; yet went he not in. Then cometh Simon Peter following him, and went into the sepulcher."

Together, they viewed the burial clothing of Jesus and saw that the napkin "that was about his head, not lying with the linen clothes, but wrapped together in a place by itself." The reality of Christ's Resurrection was not fully realized at that moment, for it is written: "For as yet they knew not the scripture, that he must rise again from the dead." Knowing that Jesus was not in the sepulchre, these presiding apostles left and "went away again unto their own home" (John 20:1-10).

Having returned again, Mary Magdalene "stood without at the sepulchre weeping." Stooping down, she looked in and saw "two angels in white sitting, the one at the head, and the other at the feet, where the body of Jesus had lain." Together, both asked Mary: "Woman, why weepest thou?" She answered: "Because they have taken away my Lord, and I know not where they have laid him" (John 20:11-13).

We do not know if other words were spoken; all that is written is that Mary turned away from the empty tomb and "saw Jesus standing, and knew not that it was Jesus."

Kindly, He asked: "Woman, why weepest thou? whom seekest thou?"

Concerned only with her own sorrow, she supposed the person speaking was the gardener. Seeking information, she earnestly asked: "Sir, if thou have borne him hence, tell me where thou hast laid him, and I will take him away."

With tenderness, Jesus said: "Mary."

That familiar voice was instantly recognized by this special woman. "She turned herself, and saith unto him, Rabboni; which is to say, Master." Her sorrow was now replaced with joy. She was the first witness that Jesus was resurrected. Instinctively she hurried to embrace Him, as doubtless she had done many times in the past.

With gentleness, Jesus says to her: "Hold me not; for I am not yet ascended to my Father; but go to my brethren, and say unto them, I ascend unto my Father, and your Father; and to my God, and your God" (John 20:14-16; Joseph Smith Translation 20:17).

Regarding this scene, Elder McConkie has written these meaningful words:

> We cannot believe," says Elder McConkie, "that the caution which withheld from Jesus the embrace of Mary was anything more than the building of a proper wall of reserve between intimates who are now on two sides of the veil . . . But perhaps there was more in Jesus' statement than Mary related or than John recorded, for in a very short time we shall see a group of faithful women hold Jesus by his feet as they worship him. The seeming refusal of Jesus to permit Mary to touch him, followed almost immediately by the appearance in which the other women were permitted to hold his feet, has always been the source of some interpretive concern. The King James Version quotes Jesus as saying 'Touch me not.' The Joseph Smith Translation reads 'Hold me not.' Various translations from the Greek render the passage as 'Do not cling to me' or 'Do not hold me.' Some give the meaning as 'Do not cling to me any longer,' or 'Do not hold me any longer.' Some speak of ceasing to hold him or cling to him, leaving the inference that Mary was already holding him. There is valid reason for supposing that the thought conveyed to Mary by the Risen Lord was to this effect: 'You cannot hold me here, for I am going to ascend to my Father.' But the great message that was preserved for us is Jesus' eternal relationship to his Father. 'My' Father and 'your' Father—Elohim is the Father of all men in the spirit, and of the Lord Jesus in an added and special

> sense. He is the Father of both Jesus' spirit and his body. 'My' God and 'your' God—and again Elohim is the God of all men, but in Jesus' case, though he himself is a God and has all power, though he is a member of the very Godhead itself, yet is he everlastingly in subjection to the same God who is our Father.[86]

Whatever else was said on this happy and glorious occasion, we are not informed. After Jesus departed, "Mary Magdalene came and told the disciples that she had seen the Lord, and that he had spoken these things unto her" (John 20:11-18).

For reasons of His own, the Risen Lord appeared first to Mary Magdalene. She was the first person to see and testify that Jesus truly was resurrected from the dead. Jesus appeared to others in that day, and they, too, testified that he lives. In our day, Joseph Smith, Jr., at age 14, saw the resurrected Lord and his resurrected Father, and they spoke to the boy-prophet (*Joseph Smith—History* 1:17). Others in our day have seen and testified that He lives.

Jacob taught that "there must needs be a power of resurrection, and the resurrection must needs come unto man by reason of the fall [of Adam and Eve and of every living thing] (2 Ne. 9:6; see also Morm. 9:12-13). In addition, it is written: "For since by man came death, by man came also the resurrection of the dead. For as in Adam all die, even so in Christ shall all be made alive" (1 Cor. 15:21-22).

Accordingly, every person will be resurrected (Alma 11:41-42; 40:2-4). However, each will not be resurrected at the same time, and each will receive varying degrees of glory (see John 5:28-29; Rev. 20; D&C 76; *Teachings*, 312).

CHAPTER SIX

Probationary Test Of Mortality

THE LIGHT OF CHRIST

When we are born in mortality, we know nothing of the Creation, the Fall, and the Atonement. We do not remember our Heavenly Parents, the Godhead, the plan of salvation, our reason for coming to earth, and of our desire to become like our Heavenly Father and His Son, Jesus Christ. There is a veil of forgetfulness placed over our mind of all that we previously knew or experienced.

Though we do not remember our prior life, we are not left without spiritual guidance on this earth during our probationary estate of mortality. Every person is endowed with the talents he or she developed in the premortal realm. In addition, all mortals are endowed with a heavenly gift called the light of Christ. At a certain age in life, every child knows right from wrong. In our language on earth, it is called a conscience. Through the Prophet Joseph Smith, the Lord says it is "the true light that lighteth every man that cometh into the world" (D&C 93:2).

Moroni explains it this way: "The Spirit of Christ is given to every man, that he may know good from evil" (Moro. 7:16). It is called "the Spirit of Jesus Christ" and "the Spirit giveth light to every man that cometh into the world" (D&C 84:45-46). It is also described as light and life and law and truth and power. It is present everywhere and is ever present. It is without shape or form or personality. Yet it is the power of God, and it is the "light which is in all things, which giveth life to all things, which is the law by which all things are governed, even the power of God who sitteth upon his throne, who is in the bosom of eternity, who is in the midst of all things" (D&C 88:13).

There is a difference between the light of Christ, the Holy Ghost, and the gift of the Holy Ghost. As has been explained, the light of Christ is ever present and gives life to all things. The Holy Ghost is the third member of the Godhead, who "is a personage of Spirit" (D&C 130:22; see also first article of faith). The gift of the Holy Ghost is received after baptism and is given by the laying on of hands by one holding priesthood authority (see D&C 35:6; 55:1; *Teachings*, 199).

Members of the Godhead use the light of Christ to fulfill their purposes. However, spiritual gifts come from God by the power of the Holy Ghost. Moroni gives this explanation: "And all these gifts come by the Spirit of Christ" (Moroni 10:17). This could mean that the Holy Ghost uses the light of Christ to transmit spiritual gifts.

Every person who is born on this earth is enlightened by the light of Christ (see D&C 93:2; John 1:4, 7-9). The light of Christ is also the light of truth. Accordingly, mankind is under the obligation to believe and seek spiritual truth. As revealed to the Prophet Joseph Smith, the Lord says: "For the word of the Lord is truth, and whatsoever is truth is light, and whatsoever is light is Spirit, even the Spirit of Jesus Christ. And the Spirit giveth light to every man that cometh into the world; and the Spirit enlighteneth every man through the world, that hearkeneth to the voice of the Spirit. And every one that hearkenth to the voice of the Spirit cometh unto God, even the Father" (D&C 84:45-47).

Therefore, if mankind hearkens to the voice of the Spirit, he will be blessed and enlightened. Truly, the light of Christ benefits all, but especially those who follow the promptings of the Holy Ghost. As such, those individuals in their probationary estate of mortality will believe the gospel message and become members of "the only true and living church upon the face of the whole earth" (D&C 1:30). By study and by the Spirit, those members will come to know the true doctrine of the Creation, the Fall, and the Atonement.

NATURAL MAN IS AN ENEMY TO GOD

In a sermon to the Nephite people, King Benjamin revealed this great truth: "For the natural man is an enemy to God, and has been from the fall of Adam, and will be, forever and ever, unless he yields to the enticings of the Holy Spirit, and putteth off the natural man and becometh a saint through the atonement of Christ the Lord, and becometh as a child" (Mosiah 3:19).

Because Adam and Eve partook of the forbidden fruit, they experienced both a physical and a spiritual death. As has been previously explained, to experience a spiritual death is to be cast out from the presence of the Lord. All of mankind has experienced this death.

Brother Hyrum Andrus has written these explanatory words: "It was only when men thereafter 'loved Satan more than God' that they began 'to be carnal, sensual, and devilish.' (Moses 5:13) It is for this reason that Joseph Smith wrote by revelation: 'But by the transgression of these holy laws . . . man became sensual and devilish, and became fallen man.' (D&C 20:20) So it is with each individual; it is only when man violates the laws of God that he becomes carnal and devilish."[87]

Though the light of Christ is given to all—to know the difference between right and wrong, and good and evil—all do not hearken to the voice of the Spirit. Many choose to walk in carnal and evil paths; they go contrary to the enticings of the Spirit.

Concerning this teaching, Elder McConkie has written this explanation:

> It is possible," says Elder McConkie, "to sear one's conscience to the point that the Spirit will withdraw its influence and men will no longer know or care about anything that is decent and edifying. 'For my Spirit shall

> not always strive with man, saith the Lord of Hosts.' (D&C 1:33) Such was the case among the Jaredites (Ether 2:15) and the Nephites (Mormon 5:16) in the day the Lord withdrew his power and left them to be destroyed by the sword. It was true among the Jews in Jerusalem when they were led away captive by Nebuchadnezzar. (1 Nephi 7:14.) It is true among any people who reject, totally and completely, the words of the apostles and prophets who are sent to them. Of our modern civilization, with all its evils and carnality, the holy word says, 'I, the Lord, am angry with the wicked; I am holding my spirit from the inhabitants of the earth.' (D&C 63:32) When the day comes that modern man is ripened in iniquity, the Spirit will cease to strive with them, and they will be destroyed by the brightness of the Lord's return.[88]

Truly, the natural man is an enemy to God. However, by listening to the promptings of the Spirit, he can overcome his carnal, sensual, and devilish ways.

THE CORRUPTIBLE STATE OF MORTALITY

The corruptible state of mortality has three meanings. First, the term is used with reference to mankind being carnal, sensual, and devilish. Using an analogy of the harvest, Paul says, "For he that soweth to his flesh shall of the flesh reap *corruption*; but he that soweth to the Spirit shall of the Spirit reap life everlasting" (Gal. 6:8; emphasis added). Thus, corruption means spiritual death. Life everlasting means eternal life (see Tim. 1:19) By sowing to the Spirit, the Saints have "escaped the corruption that is in the world through lust" (2 Peter. 1:4).

Second, mortal bodies are corruptible bodies. This means that they are subject to a natural physical decay while a person is living in mortality. Speaking of the resurrection, Abinadi said: "Even this mortal shall put on immortality, and this corruption shall put on incorruption" (Mosiah 16:10). Enoch explained: "Because that Adam fell, we are; and by his fall came death; and we are made partakers of misery and woe" (Moses 6:48). Because we have mortal bodies, we are subject to all of the afflictions and sufferings of the flesh. Though not pleasant to experience, these are essential parts of the Father's plan of salvation.

Thirdly, corruption is used to signify the decay that takes place after our mortal death. Because Adam partook of the forbidden fruit, the Lord told him: "By the sweat of thy face shalt thou eat bread, until thou shalt return unto the ground—for thou shalt surely die . . . for dust thou wast, and unto dust shalt thou return" (Moses 4:25). Excepting our Lord, who was resurrected three days after he died, most bodies experience physical corruption following death and they turn to dust.

AGENCY OF MANKIND

It is imperative to know that agency is an eternal principle and has existed throughout all eternity. As has been previously discussed, Adam and Eve were given their agency in their paradisiacal home. "Of every tree of the garden thou mayest freely eat," the Lord instructed the man and his wife, "but of the tree of the knowledge of good and evil, thou shalt not eat of it, *nevertheless, thou mayest choose for thyself, for it is given unto thee.*" (Moses 3:16-17; emphasis added). Eve willingly partook of the fruit without a full understanding of the consequences. Adam partook knowing that unless he did, he and his eternal companion could not have children and fulfill the commandment given them to multiply and replenish the earth (see Moses 2:28).

Speaking of Adam's action, Lehi said: "Adam fell that men might be; and men are, that they might have joy" (2 Ne. 2:25). It is important to emphasis that only those who gain eternal life—the life that the Father and Son enjoy—will receive a fulness of joy (see D&C 51:19).

Lehi further explains: "And the Messiah cometh in the fulness of time, that he may redeem the children of men from the fall" (2 Ne. 2:26). Thus, the Fall necessitated the Atonement; both then became essential and significant parts in the Father's plan of salvation. "And because that they [mankind] are redeemed from the fall they have become free forever, knowing good from evil; *to act for themselves* and not to be acted upon, save it be by the punishment of the law at the great and last day, according to the commandments which God hath given" (2 Ne. 2:26; emphasis added).

Giving further instruction, Lehi says: "Wherefore, men are free according to the flesh [meaning mortality]; and all things are given them which are expedient unto man. *And they are free to choose liberty and eternal life*, through the great Mediator of all men, *or to choose captivity and death,* according to the captivity and power of the devil; for he seeketh that all men might be miserable like unto himself" (2 Nephi 2:27; emphasis added).

As has been illustrated by Adam and Eve partaking of the forbidden fruit, agency was based on an opposite choice that they could have made. Again, Lehi has plainly explained: "For it must needs be, that there is an opposition in all things. If not so . . . righteousness could not be brought to pass, neither wickedness, neither holiness nor misery, neither good nor bad" (2 Ne. 2:11).

Continuing his inspired teachings, he says: ". . . for there is a God, and he hath created all things . . . and after he had created our first parents, and the beasts of the field and the fowls of the air, and in fine, all things which are created, it must needs be that there was an opposition; even the forbidden fruit in opposition to the tree of life; the one being sweet and the other bitter. Wherefore, the Lord God gave unto man that he should act for himself. Wherefore, man could not act for himself save it should be that he was enticed by the one or the other" (2 Ne. 2:14-16).

As Elder McConkie explains:

> Thus we see why the Lord gave two conflicting commandments, one to become mortal and have children, the other to not eat of the tree of knowledge of good and evil out of which mortality and children and death would result. The issue is one of choosing between

> opposites. Adam must choose to become mortal so he could have children, on the one hand; on the other hand, he must choose to remain forever in the garden in a state of innocence. He chose to partake of the forbidden fruit so that the purposes of God might be accomplished by providing a probationary estate for his spirit children. Adam must needs fall so that he would know good from evil, virtue from vice, righteousness from wickedness. He could not have done this without breaking a law and becoming subject to sin. He chose the Lord's way; there was no other way whereby salvation might come unto the children of men.[89]

With this knowledge, we turn our attention to the time in the premortal existence when God the Father presented His plan of salvation to His spirit children. When He asked whom He should send to our earth to be His Son and Redeemer, Lucifer, who is also called Satan, or the devil, offered his service, but it was based on conditions: "Behold, here am I, send me, I will be thy son, and I will redeem all mankind, that one soul shall not be lost, and surely I will do it; *wherefore give me thine honor*" (Moses 4:1; emphasis added).

As has been explained by Lehi, opposition must exist in all things, including the time spent in our premortal home. Mankind must have agency to choose good or evil, right or wrong, and most importantly salvation or damnation.

Continuing, the Lord revealed what transpired next: "But, behold, my Beloved Son, which was my Beloved and Chosen from the beginning, said unto me—Father, thy will be done, *and the glory be thine forever*" (Moses 4:2; emphasis added).

Though we do not fully know what caused Lucifer to oppose and disdain the Father and His Beloved Son, it is written: "Wherefore, because that Satan rebelled against me, *and sought to destroy the agency of man*, which I, the Lord God, had given him, and also, that I should given unto him mine own power; by the power of mine Only Begotten, I caused that he should be cast down" (Moses 4:3; emphasis added).

This is the time when there was a war in heaven, a war to preserve the agency of mankind, a war wherein one-third of the Father's spirit children followed Lucifer. Ironically, he wanted to deny mankind agency in mortality, but Lucifer and one-third of the spirit host who followed him lost their privilege to become like their Father because of their agency, which the Lord God had given them (see Rev. 12:4-9).

Through the Prophet Joseph Smith, the Lord revealed this knowledge: "And it must needs be that the devil should tempt the children of men, or they could not be agents unto themselves; for if they never should have bitter they could not know the sweet—wherefore, it came to pass that the devil tempted Adam, and he partook of the forbidden fruit and transgressed the commandment, wherein he became subject to the will of the devil, because he yielded unto temptation. Wherefore, I, the Lord God, caused that he should be cast out from the Garden of Eden, from my presence, because of his transgression, wherein he became spiritually dead." (D&C 29:39-41).

Though Adam and Eve experienced a spiritual death, they were still given agency in mortality to choose good rather than evil, to follow Satan or not, to gain eternal life or eternal damnation. Thus, mortality with all of its trials and rewards was enacted by the Fall of our first parents.

"But . . . I, the Lord God, gave unto Adam and unto his seed, that they should not die as to the temporal death, until I, the Lord God, should send forth angels to declare unto them repentance and redemption, through faith on the name of mine Only Begotten Son." Then this important doctrine is revealed: "And thus did I, the Lord God, appoint unto man the days of his probation—that by his natural death he might be raised in immortality unto eternal life, even as many as would believe; and they that believe not unto eternal damnation; for they cannot be redeemed from their spiritual fall, because they repent not" (D&C 29:42-44).

MANKIND PUNISHED FOR THEIR OWN SINS

In setting forth important teachings of the gospel, the Prophet Joseph Smith wrote the following: "We believe that men will be punished for their own sins, and not for Adam's transgression" (second article of faith). As has been explained, because mankind has agency to choose, which is based on opposition in all things, no blessings are given unless there also punishments. Adam and Eve partook of the forbidden fruit, and they paid the penalty for their transgression—both were cast out of the Garden of Eden, wherein both suffered a spiritual and a physical death.

While living in mortality, mankind is subject to laws—the laws of God, the laws of nature, and the laws of governments. Every law carries its own reward or its own punishment. Excepting our Savior, all of mankind "have sinned, and come short of the glory of God" (Romans 3:23; see also 1 John 1:8, 10). Though mankind is not required to pay for Adam's transgression, they will pay the required penalty for sin if they do not repent.

As Elder McConkie explains:

> If there were no resurrection, all men would remain subject to temporal death forever; if there were no eternal life, all men would remain spiritually dead forever; all would continue to suffer for their sins everlastingly. Hence the divine plan called for a Redeemer, for a Savior, for one who could ransom men from their fallen state, for one who would pay the penalty for their sins.[90]

THE DOCTRINE OF JUSTICE AND MERCY

Alma, the son of Alma, gives this inspired teaching to his son Corianton concerning the necessary principles of justice and mercy: "For behold, after the Lord God sent our first parents forth from the garden of Eden . . . there was a time granted unto man to repent, yea, a probationary time, a time to repent and serve God. For behold, if Adam had put forth his hand immediately, and partaken of the tree of life, he would have lived forever, according to the word of God, having no space for repentance; yea, and also the word of God would have been void, and the great plan of salvation would have been frustrated" (Alma 42:2-4).

Therefore, by Adam's transgression, a loving and merciful God allowed mankind time in mortality to exercise their agency to repent of their sins and serve him. But one asks: What happens to those individuals that die in their infancy or early childhood, for they are denied time to repent? Again, a loving and merciful God has revealed this doctrine:

"Listen to the words of Christ, your Redeemer, your Lord and your God. Behold, I came into the world not to call the righteous but sinners to repentance . . . wherefore, little children are whole, for they are not capable of committing sin; wherefore the curse of Adam [which is a spiritual death] is taken from them in me, that it hath no power over them . . . And . . . little children need no repentance, neither baptism . . . Behold I say unto you, that he that supposeth that little children need baptism is in the gall of bitterness and in the bonds of iniquity . . .

"And he that saith that little children need baptism denieth the mercies of Christ, and setteth at naught the atonement of him and the power of his redemption" (see Moroni 8:8-20).

Through the Prophet Joseph Smith, the Lord has revealed this doctrine: "No one can be received into the church of Christ unless he has arrived unto the years of accountability before God, and is capable of repentance" (D&C 20:71).

Children who develop normally become accountable "when eight years old" (D&C 68:27), and at that time, they are then subject to the law of baptism.

As Elder McConkie explains:

> Obviously if children or adults do not develop mentally to the point where they know right from wrong and have the normal intellect of an accountable person, they never arrive at the years of accountability no matter

> how many actual years they may live. Such persons, though they may be adults, are without the law, cannot repent, and are under no condemnation, 'and unto such baptism availeth nothing.' (Moro. 8:22).[91]

With this glorious doctrine stated, we return to the words of Alma: "Now, how could a man repent except he should sin? How could he sin if there was no law? How could there be a law save there was a punishment?" (Alma 42:17). His reasoning is logical and sound. "Now, there was a punishment affixed, and a just law given, which brought remorse of conscience unto man" (Alma 42:18). Thus, damnation is in large measure the remorse of conscience for sins committed and not properly repented.

"Now, if there was no law given—if a man murdered he should die—would he be afraid he would die if he should murder? And also, if there was no law given against sin men would not be afraid to sin. And if . . . men sinned what could justice do, or mercy either, for they would have no claim upon the creature?" (Alma 42:19-21). These are good questions to ponder.

"But there is a law given, and a punishment affixed, and a repentance granted [excepting those who have not reached the age of accountability]; which repentance, mercy claimeth; otherwise, justice claimeth the creature and executeth the law, and the law inflicteth the punishment; if not so, the works of justice would be destroyed, and God would cease to be God" (Alma 42:22). All of mankind commits sin; those who repent gain mercy from the Lord. For those who do not, God inflicts punishment for that particular sin.

"But God ceaseth not to be God, and mercy claimeth the penitent, and mercy cometh because of the atonement; and the atonement bringeth to pass the resurrection of the dead; and the resurrection of the dead bringeth back men into the presence of God; and thus they are restored into his presence, to be judged according to their works, according to the law and justice . . .

"What, do ye suppose that mercy can rob justice? I say unto you, Nay; not one whit. If so, God would cease to be God. And thus God bringeth about his great and eternal purposes, which were prepared from the foundation of the world. And thus cometh about the salvation and the redemption of men, and also their destruction and misery" (Alma 42:23, 25-26).

Accordingly, we know that agency, which is the law of choosing between opposites, allows for rewards and punishments for deeds done in this life. Whether or not individuals repent of their sins, mercy and justice will be exercised by a merciful and just God.

Properly understood, the probationary estate of mortality is one of the greatest blessings ever given of God to mankind. It is the only way whereby the Father's spirit children can leave their premortal home and gain mortal and then immortal bodies. Mortality provides the way for individuals to exercise agency and to be rewarded or punished for their own sins. It is therefore an essential and critical time to prepare the faithful for eternal life and exaltation (see D&C 76:5-6, 50-70).

CHAPTER SEVEN

The Strait and Narrow Path

THE TALENT TO BELIEVE

From the days of Adam to our time, there have been a myriad of religious beliefs. In addition to millions of individuals who belong to various Christian denominations in this world, there are billions who believe in Buddhism, hedonism, Hinduism, Scientism, Shintoism, and an assortment of other religions.

There are numberless people who do not believe in organized religion or that there is a Supreme Being—even the Father and God of us all. In large measure, these various beliefs are influenced on earth by a common culture, tradition, or kinship. Because of the eternal principle of agency, each individual is free to believe as he or she will.

"Why is it easy for some people," says Elder McConkie, "to believe in Christ, in his prophets, and in his gospel? Why do others reject the gospel, persecute the prophets, and even deny the divinity of Him whose gospel it is? Jesus said: 'I am the good shepherd, and know my sheep, and am known of mine . . . My sheep hear my voice, and I know them, and they follow me.' (John 10:14, 27)

"From [this] and a host of other passages, it is clear that people do not all have the same talent for recognizing truth and believing the doctrines of salvation. Some heed the warning voice and believe the gospel; others do not. Some would give all they possess if they could but touch the hem of the garment of him who is the Way, the Truth, and the Life; others find fault with every word that falls from prophetic lips. Some forsake lands and riches, friends and families, to gather with the true saints; others choose to walk in the ways of the world and to deride the humble followers of Christ. Why? Why this difference in people?"

Continuing, he provides this explanation:

"To this problem there is no easy answer. Every person stands alone in choosing his beliefs and electing the course he will pursue. No two persons are born with the same talents and capacities; no two are rooted in the same soil of circumstances; each is unique. The cares of this world, gold and honor and power and renown, the lusts of the flesh, the chains of past sins, and a thousand other things—all exert their influence upon us. But in the final sense the answer stems back to premortality. We all lived as spirit beings, as children of the Eternal Father, for an infinitely long period of time in the premortal existence. There we developed talents, gifts, and aptitudes; there our capacities and abilities took form; there, by obedience to law, we were endowed with the power, in one degree or another, to believe the truth and follow the promptings of the Spirit. And the talent of greatest worth was that of spirituality, for it enables us to hearken to the Holy Spirit and accept the gospel which prepares us for eternal life."

He then concludes:

"Men are not born equal. They enter this life with the talents and capacities developed in preexistence . . .

"And as it is with the prophets, so is it with all the chosen seed. 'God's elect,' as Paul call them (Romans 8:33), are especially endowed at birth with spiritual talents. It is easier for them to believe the gospel than it is for the generality of mankind. Every living soul comes into this world with sufficient talent to believe and be saved, but the Lord's sheep, as a reward for their devotion when they dwelt in his presence, enjoy greater spiritual endowments than their fellows . . . ."[92]

As has been written, there are degrees of belief, and they were obtained by the talents and capacities developed in the premortal existence. Thus, to believe in the true teachings and doctrines as set forth by the Lord and his chosen servants will bring salvation.

Those who believe in a false system of salvation will not gain exaltation in the highest degree of glory (see D&C 76). Therefore, salvation can only come to those who believe the true gospel of Jesus Christ. That is why missionary work—to teach by example and precept throughout mortal life—is required of every member of the Church of Jesus Christ of Latter-day Saints (see D&C 4). To those who do not fulfill their missionary obligation, the Lord has stated: "But with some I am not well pleased, for they will not open their mouths, but they hide the talent which I have given unto them, because of the fear of man. Wo unto such, for mine anger is kindled against them" (D&C 60:2).

But what of all those people who have not heard the gospel message, both before the Lord's ministry on earth and those who do not have an opportunity in this life up to the time of the Millennium reign? To answer, we turn to a vision given to President Joseph F. Smith, sixth President of the Church, wherein he says:

> And I wondered at the words of Peter—wherein he said that the Son of God preached unto the spirits in prison, who sometime were disobedient, when once the long-suffering of God waited in the days of Noah—and how it was possible for him to preach to those spirits and perform the necessary labor among them in so short a time.

He then reveals his vision:

> And as I wondered, my eyes were opened, and my understanding quickened, and I perceived that the Lord went not in person among the wicked and the disobedient who had rejected the truth, to teach them; but behold, from among the righteous, he organized his forces and appointed messengers, clothed with power and authority, and commissioned them to go forth and carry the light of the gospel to them that were in darkness, even to all the spirits of men; and thus was the gospel preached to the dead . . .

This doctrine is then set forth:

> These were taught faith in God, repentance from sin, vicarious baptism for the remission of sins, the gift of the Holy Ghost by the laying on of hands, and all other principles of the gospel that were necessary for them to know in order to qualify themselves that they might be judged according to men in the flesh, but live according to God in the spirit.

He then concludes:

> And so it was made known among the dead, both small and great, the unrighteous as well as the faithful, that redemption had been wrought through the sacrifice of the Son of God upon the cross" (D&C 138:28-30, 33-35).

Therefore, to believe the true teachings and doctrines as set forth by the Lord and His chosen servants will bring salvation. We fervently pray that mankind—no matter his religious affiliation or views—will have the ability to believe the true gospel message, which consists of "the doctrine of the resurrection and the redemption of mankind from the fall, and from individual sins on conditions of repentance" (D&C 138:19). And, I solemnly testify that these saving truths can only be found in The Church of Jesus Christ of Latter-day Saints.

TO ACT FOR OURSELVES

From our time in the premortal existence to our present state in mortality, we have been given agency. Thus, opposition to choose right or wrong, good or bad, eternal life or eternal damnation is essential to the purposes of our lives. As Lehi has explained: "And to bring about his eternal purposes . . . the Lord God gave unto man that he should act for himself. Wherefore, man could not act for himself save it should be that he was enticed by the one or the other" (2 Ne. 2:15-16).

Every person who is born on this earth is given the light of Christ—to know right from wrong. How they choose to feel and think and act will determine how their lives will be influenced for good or bad. Though myriads of people in the world do not believe the doctrine of the Godhead—consisting of God the Father, His Beloved Son, Jesus Christ, and the Holy Ghost—They are indeed a reality (first article of faith). This truth has been revealed by the Prophet Joseph Smith (see *Joseph Smith—History* 1:17).

Concerning the Lord's role in preserving our agency, Lehi again taught: "And the Messiah cometh in the fulness of time, that he may redeem the children of men from the fall. And because that they are redeemed from the fall they have become free forever, knowing good from evil; *to act for themselves and not to be acted upon. . .*" (2 Ne. 2:26). This is a significant statement!

In our probationary estate of mortality, we must avoid being acted upon by acting for ourselves to avoid evil. To be "free forever," we must choose right over wrong, truth over untruth, to follow the correct teachings of the Savior over not following them. The list can go on.

Thus, in mortality, there are many things to act and things to be acted upon. All of us are sons and daughters of our Heavenly Father, and each has been blessed with the gift of moral agency, the capacity for independent action and choice. Though we have agency to choose how we will live, we are not free to suffer or not suffer the consequences for unwise choices.

To illustrate: Those who smoke, take drugs, or drink alcoholic beverages have their agency to do so, but they cannot avoid the consequences of health risks and possible death. By their actions, they also forfeit their right to the promptings of the Holy Ghost. Those who use their agency to disobey traffic laws must suffer the consequences for their actions.

Those who use their agency to believe the true teachings and doctrines as set forth by the Lord and His chosen servants will gain salvation. Those who use their agency to believe otherwise risk the consequences of damnation (see D&C 76). Thus, during our sojourn in mortality, we must be wise with our agency to act for ourselves in righteousness and not to be acted upon by the consequences of unrighteous choices.

CONVERSION

Those individuals who have the talent to believe the truth and become members of The Church of Jesus Christ of Latter-day Saints are called converts. Whether one is born to members of the Church or whether one is converted to the Church by missionary effort, each must gain his or her own testimony of the truthfulness of the gospel. Therefore, conversion is a personal and essential matter.

As Elder McConkie explains:

> In the full gospel sense . . . conversion is more—far more—than merely changing one's belief from that which is false to that which is true; it is more than the acceptance of the verity of gospel truths, than the acquirement of a testimony. To convert is to change from one status to another, and gospel conversion consists in the transformation of man from his fallen and carnal state to a state of saintliness.[93]

Speaking to members of the Church, President Harold B. Lee made this observation:

> To become converted, according to the scriptures, meant having a change of heart and the moral character of a person turned from the controlled power of sin into a righteous life.

He then makes this interesting but truth-filled declaration:

> Conversion must mean more than just being a 'card carrying' member of the Church with a tithing receipt, a membership card, a temple recommend, etc. It means to overcome the tendencies to criticize and to strive continually to improve inward weaknesses and not merely the outward appearances.[94]

There are many conversion stories—some are recorded in the scriptures, others are from family and friends. Each conversion is unique and special. With this stated, we again use the words of President Harold B. Lee:

> What does it mean to become converted? . . . The testimony you have today will not be your testimony of tomorrow. Your testimony is either going to grow and grow until it becomes as the brightness of the sun, or it is going to diminish to nothing, depending on what we do about it . . .

He then makes this declaration:

> One is converted when he sees with his eyes what he ought to see; when he hears with his ears what he ought to hear; and when he understands with his heart what he ought to understand—then he is converted. But when he fails to see, and fails to hear, and fails to understand for some reason, that man has lost his faith. He has lost his testimony, because of something he has done.[95]

As members of the Church, we must continually be converted to the gospel of Jesus Christ. We must follow the counsel and teachings of the Lord's chosen servants (see D&C 1:38). We must continually use our agency to be good instead of being evil. We have been given the blessings of the priesthood, of missionary work, of genealogy work, of the temple, and the saving truths of the gospel. We know the true doctrine of the Godhead, of the Creation, the Fall, and the Atonement.

We know that the gospel was restored in these latter days through the Prophet Joseph Smith (see D&C 1:17). We have the light of Christ and the gift of the Holy Ghost to bless our lives and lead us in the paths of righteousness.

Truly, we are blessed by our conversion. And truly our salvation and exaltation depends on our staying converted to the gospel of Jesus Christ to the end of our mortal lives.

FAITH, GRACE, AND WORKS

Since the days of the Reformation there seems to be among the Christian denominations a controversy over faith, grace, and works. Writing to the Ephesians, Paul the apostle wrote: "*For by grace are ye saved through faith*; and that not of yourselves: it is the gift of God; *Not of works*, lest any man should boast" (Eph. 2:8-9; emphasis added).

James, the Lord's brother, who also was called to be an apostle, wrote to the saints of his day: "Yea, a man may say, Thou hast faith, and I have works: shew me thy faith without thy works, and I will shew thee my faith by my works. Thou believest that there is one God; thou doest well: the devils also believe, and tremble. But wilt thou know, O vain man, *that faith without works is dead*?" (James 2:18-20; emphasis added).

Concerning these two passages of scripture, wherein there seems to be a difference in doctrine, we turn to the words of then Elder Joseph Fielding Smith for clarification:

> I desire to point out wherein there is no conflict whatever in the teachings of these two apostles of old; that Paul taught the doctrine that was taught by James; and James was in full accord with the doctrine that was taught by Paul—the fact being that they were approaching the subject from different angles.

Writing of the statement of Paul, he says:

> Paul was dealing with the class of people [the Ephesians] who believed that a man could not be saved unless he subscribed to the *law of Moses*, that a man was under the necessity more or less of saving himself, and who denied the full power of the atonement of Jesus Christ.

Writing of the statement of James, he says:

> James on the other hand [while speaking to the saints of his day] was defending the necessity of works,

counteracting the idea which prevailed among *others*, who professed faith in Christ, that if they had faith it was all-sufficient. Therefore they approached this subject from different viewpoints, and each of them taught the truth.

He then logically provides this information:

> So Paul taught these people—who thought that they could be saved by some power that was within them, or by observing the law of Moses—he pointed out to them the fact that if it were not for the mission of Jesus Christ, if it were not for this great atoning sacrifice, they could not be redeemed. And therefore *it was by the grace of God that they are saved,* not by any work on their part, for they were absolutely helpless. Paul was absolutely right.
>
> And on the other hand, James taught just as the Lord taught, just as Paul had taught in other scripture, that it is our duty, of necessity, to labor, to strive in diligence, and faith, keeping the commandments of the Lord, if we would obtain that inheritance which is promised to the faithful, and which shall be given unto them through their faithfulness to the end."

Elder Smith then gives his personal belief:

> So it is easy to understand that we must accept the mission of Jesus Christ. We must believe that it is through his grace that we are saved, that he performed for us that labor which we were unable to perform for ourselves, and did for us those things which were essential to our salvation, which were beyond our power; and also that we are under the commandment and the necessity of performing the labors that are required of us as set forth in the commandments known as the gospel of Jesus Christ.

He then concludes:

> Unless a man will adhere to the doctrine and walk in faith, accepting the truth and observing the commandments as they have been given, it will be impossible for him to receive eternal life, no matter how much he may confess with his lips that Jesus is the Christ, or believe that his Father sent him into the world for the redemption of man. So James is right when he says the devils 'believe and tremble,' but they do not repent. So it is necessary, not merely that we believe, but that we repent, and in faith perform good works until the end; and then shall we receive the reward of the faithful and a place in the celestial kingdom of God.[96]

Be it known that salvation can only come by faith, grace, and works and these fundamental doctrines are inseparably woven together. And be it known that they are operational in their fulness only with those individuals who are active members of The Church of Jesus Christ of Latter-day Saints to end of their mortal life.

THE STRAIT AND NARROW PATH

In the Book of Mormon, we are informed of a vision that Lehi and his son Nephi were both privileged to see. Without relating the entire vision, we will emphasize a few items: Both of these righteous men noticed a rod of iron extending along the riverbank and leading to a tree where he stood. Beside the iron rod *was a strait and narrow path*, leading also to this tree. The tree, whose fruit was sweet and agreeable, represents the tree of life or the love of God. The rod of iron represents the word of God. The numberless concourses of people pressing forward toward *the strait and narrow path* leading to the tree seem to represent the people of the world whose intentions and desires are good. (see 1 Ne. 8:19-23; 1 Ne. 11:8, 25, 33; emphasis added).

Later in his record, this same Nephi revealed this doctrine:

"And now, my beloved brethren, I know by this that unless a man shall endure to the end, in following the example of the Son of the living God, he cannot be saved. Wherefore, do the things which

I have told you I have seen that your Lord and Redeemer should do . . . that ye might know the gate by which ye should enter. For the gate by which ye should enter is repentance and baptism by water; and then cometh a remission of your sins by fire and by the Holy Ghost. *And then are ye in this strait and narrow path which leads to eternal life*" (2 Ne. 31:16-18; emphasis added).

In the Book of Mormon both the words "strait" and "straight" are used. In the vision that Lehi and Nephi saw, they saw this "*strait* and narrow path which leads to eternal life" (see 1 Ne. 8:20; 2 Ne. 31:28; emphasis added). However, this same Nephi writes: "O then, my beloved brethren, come unto the Lord, the Holy One. Remember that his paths are righteousness. Behold, the way for man is narrow, but it lieth in a *straight* course before him. . ." (2 Ne. 9:41; emphasis added). Thus, both the words "strait" and "straight" are written.

Three years before his death, Elder McConkie gave one of the most comforting and faith-promoting speeches of his life. In his talk, he uses the word "straight" to speak of the path leading to eternal life. Says he:

"This is a true gospel verity—that everyone in the church who is on the straight and narrow path, who is striving and struggling and desiring to do what is right, though is far from perfect in this life; if he passes out of this life while he's on the straight and narrow, he's going to go on to eternal reward in his Father's kingdom.

"We don't need to get a complex or get a feeling that you have to be perfect to be saved. You don't. There's only been one perfect person, and that's the Lord Jesus, but in order to be saved in the Kingdom of God and in order to pass the test of mortality, *what you have to do is get on the straight and narrow path*—thus charting a course leading to eternal life—*and then, being on that path, pass out of this life in full fellowship*. I'm not saying that you don't have to keep the commandments. I'm saying you don't have to be perfect to be saved. If you did, no one would be saved. *The way it operates is this: you get on the path that's name the 'straight and narrow.' You do it by entering the gate of repentance and baptism. The straight and narrow path leads from the gate of repentance and baptism, a very great distance, to a reward that's called eternal life. If you're on that path and pressing forward, and you die, you'll never get off the path.* There is no such thing as falling off the straight and narrow path in the life to come, and the reason is that this life is the time that is given to men to prepare for eternity. Now is the time and the day of your salvation, so if you're working zealously in this life—though you haven't fully overcome the world and you haven't done all you hoped you might do—you're still going to be saved. You don't have to do what Jacob said, 'Go beyond the mark.' You don't have to live a life that's truer than true. You don't have to have an excessive zeal that becomes fanatical and unbalancing. What you have to do is stay in the mainstream of the church and live as upright and decent people live in the Church—keeping the commandments, paying your tithing, serving in the organizations of the Church, loving the Lord, staying on the straight and narrow path. If you're on that path when death comes—because this is the time and the day appointed, this is the probationary estate—you'll never fall off from it, and, for all practical purposes, your calling and election is made sure."[97]

Because of the eternal plan of salvation, God the Father and his Beloved Son, Jesus Christ, have restored the gospel in our dispensation through the Prophet Joseph Smith, which provides the only way that mankind can come back into their presence and become like them (see D&C 1:17-30; *Joseph Smith—History* 1:17-20; D&C 76).

With the talent to believe the truth, using agency to act for ourselves, by becoming converted to The Church of Jesus Christ of Latter-day Saints, and working by faith and works, we are on the "straight and narrow path" that leads to eternal life. It is my fervent prayer that we will endure to the end of our mortal life on this path so that we are saved by the grace of God.

CONCLUSION

To briefly reiterate what has been presented in this work, I solemnly declare that God, who is our Heavenly Father, came to earth and created Adam and Eve in His own image and likeness. The earth was first created in a paradisiacal state so that there could be a Fall. Christ became our Savior and Redeemer, so that He could ransom mankind from the effects of the fall. By our Lord's Atonement and resurrection mankind might gain immortality and eternal life, based upon their faithfulness.

Thus, the Father of us all ordained and established a plan of salvation whereby his spirit children might advance and become like Him. It is the gospel of God, the plan of the Eternal Father, the only way that mankind can be saved and exalted. It consists of the three most important events in all the eternities—the Creation, the Fall, and the Atonement. Now we know how they are inseparably connected together.

Notes

CHAPTER ONE

1 Joseph Smith, *Teachings of the Prophet Joseph Smith*, sel. Joseph Fielding Smith (Salt Lake City: Deseret Book, 1938) 48; hereafter referred to as *Teachings*.

2 Bruce R. McConkie, *A New Witness for the Articles of Faith* (Salt Lake City: Deseret Book, 1985), 81; hereafter referred to as *A New Witness*.

3 Smith, *Teachings*, 342-345.

4 Ibid., 345.

5 Ibid., 345-346.

6 Ibid., p. 373; *Discourses of Brigham Young*, sel. John A. Widtsoe (Salt Lake City: Deseret book, 1954) 22.

7 Smith, *Teachings*, 354.

8 McConkie, *A New Witness*, p. 51.

9 Smith, *Teachings*, p. 190.

10 In *Journal of Discourses*, 26 vols. (London: Latter-day Saints' Book Depot, 1854-86) 26: 196-197.

11 Bruce R. McConkie, *Mormon Doctrine*, 2nd ed. (Salt Lake City: Bookcraft, 1966) 516; hereafter referred to as *Mormon Doctrine*.

12 Ibid., 516.

13 Spencer W. Kimball, in *Conference Reports of The Church of Jesus Christ of Latter-day Saints* (Salt Lake City: The Church of Jesus Christ of Latter-day Saints, 1898 to present), April 1, 1978, 7.

14 Gordon B. Hinckley, of the First Presidency, An Address, April 5, 1991, Regional Representative Seminar, 3.

15 Smith, *Teachings*, 300-301.

16 Smith, *Teachings*, 353; Abraham 3; Moses 1-4; McConkie, Mormon Doctrine, 589-590.

17 Smith, *Teachings*, 158; In *Journal of Discourses*, 26 vols. (London: Latter-day Saints' Book Depot, 1854-86) 6:310; hereafter referred to as *Journal of Discourses*.

18 Smith, *Teachings*, 353.

19 McConkie, *Mormon Doctrine*, 76-77.

20 Ibid., p. 387.

21 Speaking of all the worlds that were created by the Savior, the Prophet Joseph Smith says, "Whose inhabitants, too, from the first to the last . . . ." *Millennial Star*, 4:49-55; as written in *Mormon Doctrine*, 66.

22 Bruce R. McConkie, *The Mortal Messiah: From Bethlehem to Calvary*, 4 vols. (Salt Lake City: Deseret Book, 1979) 1:29.

23 Ibid., footnote 7, 32-33.

24 Ibid., 29-30.

25 Smith, *Teachings*, 190.

26 McConkie, *A New Witness*, 68.

CHAPTER TWO

27 Joseph Fielding Smith, *Doctrines of Salvation*, comp. Bruce R. McConkie, 3 vols. (Salt Lake City: Bookcraft, 1954-56), 1:75. Hereafter referred to as *Doctrines of Salvation*.

28 Ibid., 75-76.

29 Smith, *Teachings*, pp. 350-352.

30 *Doctrines of Salvation*, 1:79.

31 *Journal of Discourses*, 7:285.

32 Orson F. Whitney, *Improvement Era*, 30 (August 1927) 855.

33 Smith, *Teachings*, 291-292.

34 Joseph Smith, *History of the Church of Jesus Christ of Latter-day Saints*, ed. B. H. Roberts, 2d ed. rev., 7 vols. (Salt Lake City: The Church of Jesus Christ of Latter-day Saints, 1932-51) 6:476.

35 *Deseret News Semi-Weekly*, no. 54 (26 August 1915) 9.

36 *Course of study for Priests-1910*; prepared and issued under the direction of the General Authorities of the Church—December 4, 1909. The General Committee consists of Rudger Clawson, David O. McKay, Seymour B.

Young, B. H. Roberts, Rulon S. Wells, Joseph W. McMurrin, Charles W. Nibley, etc., p. 37.

37 Joseph F. Smith, John R. Winder, Anthon H. Lund, *Improvement Era,* 13 (November 1909) 80.

38 Joseph Fielding Smith, *Man: His Origin And Destiny,* (Salt Lake City: Deseret Book, 1954) 343-345. Also found in: *Messages of the First Presidency,* 4:266.

39 *Journal of Discourses,* 15:137.

40 McConkie, *Mormon Doctrine,* 742.

CHAPTER THREE

41 Smith, *Teachings,* 38-39, 157-158, 167.

42 Ibid., p. 297; McConkie, *Mormon Doctrine,* 828.

43 Smith, *Teachings,* 157.

44 Smith, *Doctrines of Salvation,* 1956, 3:74.

45 *The Historical Record,* Andrew Jenson, Vol. 7 and 8: 432; Orson F. Whitney, *Life of Heber C. Kimball,* 1888 ed., 219; as printed in Alvin R. Dyer, *The Refiner's Fire,* (Salt Lake City: Deseret Book1969) 111.

46 *Life of John D. Lee,* 91, as printed in *The Refiner's Fire,* 10.

47 Smith, *Doctrines of Salvation,* 1956, 3:77.

48 Smith, *Doctrines of Salvation,* 1954, 1:26, 103-104.

49 Smith, *Doctrines of Salvation,* 1955, 2:71.

50 Joseph Fielding Smith, *Man: His Origin And Destiny,* (Salt Lake City: Deseret Book, 1954) 383-384; also in John Taylor, *The Government of God,* 106-115; Parley P. Pratt, *The Voice of Warning,* (Salt Lake City: George Q. Cannon & Sons Co., 1891 ed.) 135-136.

51 Hyrum L Andrus, *Doctrinal Commentary on the Pearl of Great Price,* (Salt Lake City: Deseret Book, 1970) 204-205; hereafter referred to as Andrus.

52 McConkie, *Mormon Doctrine,* 804.

53 Milton R. Hunter, *Pearl of Great Price Commentary,* (Salt Lake City: Bookcraft, 1971) 118; hereafter referred to as Hunter; McConkie, *Mormon Doctrine,* 268-269.

54 McConkie, *Mormon Doctrine,* 289.

55 Hunter, 119.

56 McConkie, *A New Witness,* 87.

CHAPTER FOUR

57 *Times and Seasons* [Nauvoo, Illinois], 6 Vols. 1839-1846; this quotation was written February 1, 1842, 3:672; also written in Andrus, 200.

58 Bruce R. McConkie, *Christ and the Creation,* Ensign, June, 1982, 3-4.

59 Alvin R. Dyer, *The Refiner's Fire,* (Salt Lake City: Deseret Book, 1969) 110; Elder Dyer is quoting *Life of John D. Lee,* 91.

60 McConkie, *Mormon Doctrine,* 19-20.

61 Ibid., 20.

62 Ibid., 21.

CHAPTER FIVE

63 Smith, *Teachings,* 121.

64 McConkie, *Mormon Doctrine,* 64-65.

65 James E. Talmage, *Jesus the Christ* (Salt Lake City: Deseret Book, 1962), 610-611, 620; herafter referred to as *Jesus the Christ.*

66 Bruce R. McConkie, *The Mortal Messiah: From Bethlehem to Calvary,* Book 4, (Salt Lake City: Deseret Book, 1981) 125; hereafter referred to as *The Mortal Messiah.*

67 Ibid., 125.

68 Ibid. 124.

69 McConkie, *Doctrinal New Testament Commentary,* Vol. 1, The Gospels (Salt Lake City: Bookcraft, 1965) 774-775.

70 Talmage, *Jesus the Christ,* 613-614.

71 Ibid., 661.

72 McConkie, *The Mortal Messiah,* Book 4, 227-228.

73 Talmage, *Jesus the Christ,* Note 8, 668-669.

74 McConkie, *The Mortal Messiah,* Book 4, 261-262; Elder McConkie is quoting a Jewish Scholar, Alfred Edersheim, Book 2:630-631.

75 McConkie, *The Mortal Messiah,* Book 4, 264-265.

CHAPTER SIX

76 Andrus, 213.

77 McConkie, *A New Witness*, 260.

78 Ibid., 91.

79 Ibid., 94.

80 McConkie, *Mormon Doctrine*, 853.

CHAPTER SEVEN

81 McConkie, *A New Witness*, 33-35.

82 McConkie, *Mormon Doctrine*, 162.

83 Harold B. Lee, *Conference Report*, April 4, 1971, 92.

84 Harold B. Lee, An Address, September 27, 1971, Brigham Young University "Laurels" Fireside, 11.

85 Smith, *Doctrines of Salvation*, Vol.2, 307-311.

86 Bruce R. McConkie, *The Probationary Test Of Mortality*, University of Utah, 10 January 1982, 12-13.

INDEX

ABOUT THE AUTHOR

Bruce E. Dana is an avid student of the gospel, who served as a missionary in the Northwestern States and Pacific Northwest missions for the Church. He attended Weber State College and Utah State University. Brother Dana has served in a wide variety of Church callings and enjoys teaching the doctrines of the gospel. He is married to Brenda Lamb and is the father of eight children.

Brother Dana is the author of seven other LDS doctrinal books, as well as the bestselling humor book *Stories and Jokes of Mormon Folks*.